WORLD BOOK'S

YOUNG SCIENTIST

WORLD BOOK'S

YOUNG SCIENTIST

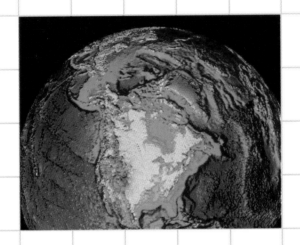

- • PLANET EARTH
- • WATER

6

World Book, Inc.
a Scott Fetzer company
Chicago

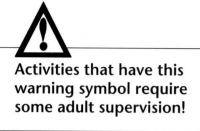

Activities that have this warning symbol require some adult supervision!

The quest to explore the known world and to describe its creation and subsequent development is nearly as old as mankind. In the Western world, the best-known creation story comes from the book of Genesis. It tells how God created Earth and all living things. Modern religious thinkers interpret the Biblical story of creation in various ways. Some believe that creation occurred exactly as Genesis describes it. Others think that God's method of creation is revealed through scientific investigation. *Young Scientist* presents an exciting picture of what scientists have learned about life and the universe.

World Book, Inc.
233 N. Michigan Avenue
Chicago, IL 60601

For information on other World Book products, call 1-800-WORLDBK (967-5325), or visit us at our Web site at http://www.worldbook.com

© 1997, 1995, 1991, 1990 World Book, Inc.

ISBN: 0-7166-2756-6 (volume VI)
ISBN: 0-7166-2797-3 (set)

Library of Congress Catalog Card No. 00-107193

Printed in the United States of America

1 2 3 4 5 6 7 06 05 04 03 02 01 00

Contents

Planet Earth

Water

PLANET EARTH

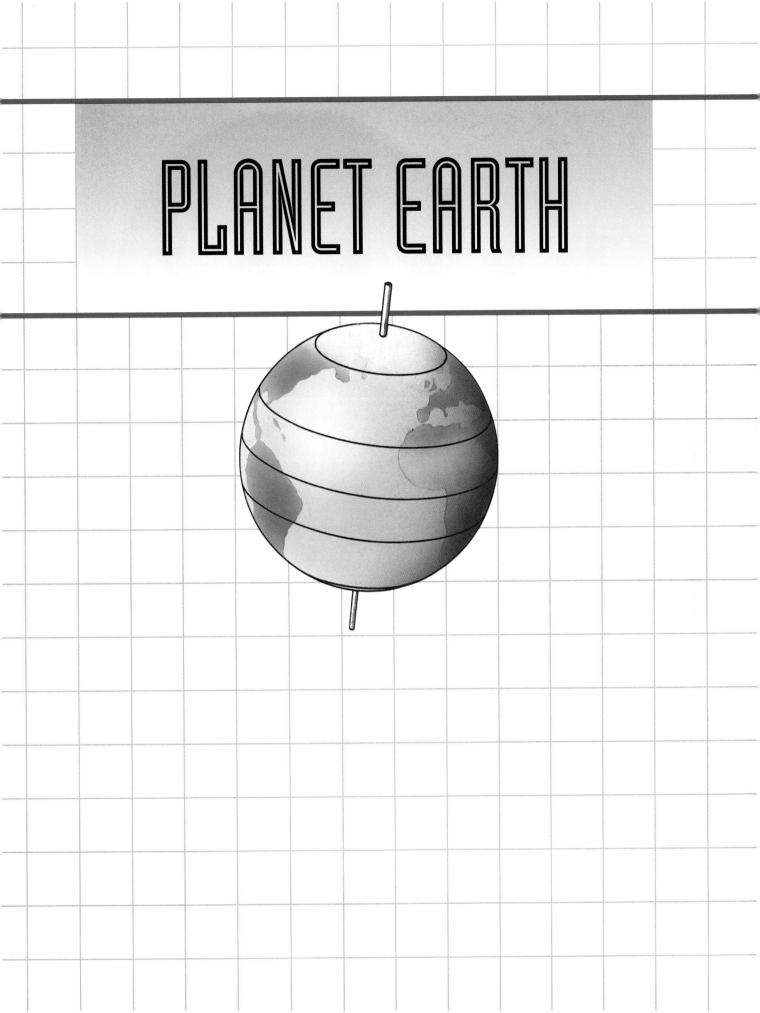

Our planet Earth

Imagine you are an astronaut traveling in a spaceship to the moon. After you rise far above Earth's surface and look back at it, what do you think you would see? Astronauts who have been to the moon say Earth looks like a blue ball shining in a black sky. Earth's surface is often covered with enormous patches of swirling, white clouds.

The blue color comes from the oceans of our planet. The black sky is the emptiness of outer space. From your astronauts' base on the moon, Earth would look very small! But if you could dig your way straight to Earth's middle, your tunnel would be almost 4,000 miles (6,400 kilometers) long!

Water, land, and air

Our planet is one of nine planets that go around the sun. All the planets receive energy from the sun, but Earth is the only planet believed to support living things. These living things inhabit all the corners of the planet—its water, land, and air.

Most of Earth's surface is covered by seas and oceans. About one quarter of the surface is dry land, with various kinds of landscapes. These may be deserts, forests, grasslands, or mountains. Or the land may be covered by ice, like Antarctica. And all around Earth there is the **atmosphere.** This is made up of several layers of air, which contain mixtures of different gases.

*This is the view of Earth astronauts
see from the moon.*

When Earth began

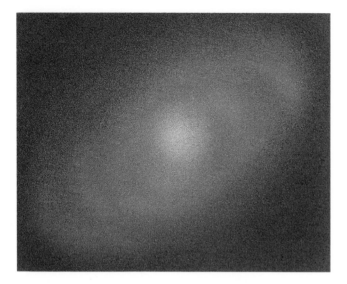

A cloud of gas and dust

How old is Earth? No one really knows. Our planet is part of the **solar system**, which is made up of the sun and all the objects that travel around it. Scientists think that our solar system began about 4.6 billion years ago. At that time, a gigantic cloud of gas and dust spun around like a huge flat wheel, millions and millions of miles (kilometers) across. Most of the gas in this cloud, or **nebula**, was hydrogen.

The beginning of the sun

During thousands of millions of years, the shape of the nebula was changed by **gravity**. This is a force that pulls things toward each other.

The gravity of the spinning nebula pulled gas and dust into the center, creating a tightly packed lump. This massive lump was shaped like a ball and was the beginning of the star we call the **sun.**

Life on Earth

Think of the time since Earth began as being equal to the 12 months of the year. The first humans would then have appeared at 5 p.m. on the last day of December.

The sun's heat and light provide energy throughout our solar system, but Earth is the only planet on which we know there is life. Animals and plants survive on Earth because the planet is warm and the atmosphere is full of air to breathe. The atmosphere also provides protection from certain harmful rays of the sun.

1. The solar system formed 4.6 billion years ago.

2. Life on Earth began 3.5 billion years ago.

3. Amebas (one-celled organisms) appeared 3 billion years ago.

1.			2.		3.		
January	February	March	April		May		June

The sun shines brightly

As the new star grew larger and became more tightly packed, the gas at its center became very hot. The heat was so great that it started a series of nuclear **reactions**, or changes, like those inside a nuclear bomb. These continuing reactions cause the sun to shine.

The solar system forms

Many scientists believe Earth formed about 4.5 billion years ago. Far away from the shining sun, the force of gravity began to pull gas and dust into much smaller centers, like whirlpools in space. Over millions of years, these also became tightly packed balls of gas and dust. Today, we know them as the nine planets of our solar system, all still traveling around the sun.

Scientists believe that life on our planet began about 3.5 billion years ago—that's only 1 billion years after Earth formed. The first plants and animals lived in the oceans. Then, over 400 million years ago, living things appeared on dry land. Dinosaurs appeared 200 million years ago. Human beings didn't develop until about 2 million years ago.

7. The first type of human being appeared about 2 million years ago.

6. Dinosaurs lived on Earth from about 200 million years ago to about 65 million years ago.

4. The first fish appeared about 500 million years ago.

5. Living things began to appear on dry land 400 million years ago.

July	August	September	October	November	December
				4.	5.	6.	7.

What is Earth made of?

How do we know what is inside Earth? Astronauts have traveled about 228,000 miles (380,000 kilometers) above Earth's surface, but no one has ever been able to go very far beneath it.

The deepest mine that humans have ever dug is less than 2.4 miles (4 kilometers) deep, and the longest drill on an oil rig reaches less than 4.8 miles (8 kilometers). But the center of our planet lies much deeper, about 4,000 miles (6,400 kilometers) below the surface of Earth!

If you could cut a wedge out of Earth, you would be able to see the different layers beneath Earth's surface.

**800 miles
(1,300 kilometers) thick**

**1,400 miles
(2,250 kilometers) thick**

**1,800 miles
(2,900 kilometers) thick**

**19 miles
(32 kilometers) thick**

The **inner core** is the hottest part of Earth. It is very heavy because most of it is made of iron and nickel.

The **outer core** is made of hot, liquid rocks containing iron, nickel, and other elements.

The **mantle** contains mostly heavy rocks. In the deepest part of the mantle, these rocks melt because of very high temperatures.

The **crust** is a hard, rocky shell around Earth. It consists mostly of two types of rock—granite and basalt.

Inside Earth

Earth's outer layer is called the **crust.** If Earth were an apple, the crust would be its skin.

The crust that lies under the oceans is mostly made of a rock called **basalt.** It is about 5 miles (8 kilometers) thick. The large areas of Earth's crust that are not covered by oceans are mostly made of a rock called **granite.** These areas are what we call land. They are the **continents** and **islands** of the planet.

The continental crust is usually about 19 miles (32 kilometers) thick. In some places, where there are high mountain ranges, it can be more than 25 miles (40 kilometers) thick. Underneath its crust, Earth is made up of three layers of hot rocks and metals. These layers are called the **mantle,** the **outer core,** and the **inner core.**

The mantle is the layer of rock below the crust. It is 1,800 miles (2,900 kilometers) thick. At its deepest point, the mantle has a temperature as high as 8000 °F (4400 °C)—hot enough to melt iron! Some of the rocks here are so hot that they are liquid, or **molten.** Under the mantle lies the outer core. This is made of molten rocks. The outer core has a temperature ranging from 8000 °F (4400 °C) to about 11,000 °F (6100 °C). It is about 1,400 miles (2,250 kilometers) thick.

At Earth's center

Earth's center is called the inner core. It is about 800 miles (1,300 kilometers) thick. Scientists believe that it is ball-shaped and made of two types of metal, iron and **nickel.** Here, the temperature is as high as 13,000 °F (7000 °C). But the metals remain solid. This is because of the enormous weight caused by the other layers pressing down on top of them.

Find out more by looking at pages **38–39**

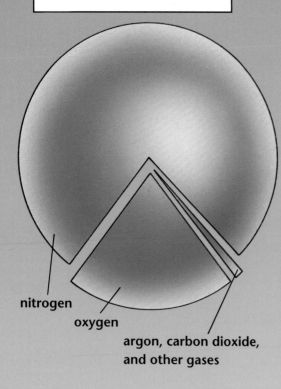

nitrogen

oxygen

argon, carbon dioxide, and other gases

The troposphere is a mixture of gases. Nearly four-fifths is nitrogen. About one-fifth is oxygen, and the rest is made up of argon, carbon dioxide, and other gases.

What is in the atmosphere?

Several layers of air surround our planet. Together, these are known as the **atmosphere.** The layer nearest Earth's surface is called the **troposphere.** It is about 6 miles (10 kilometers) thick at the poles and 10 miles (16 kilometers) thick at the equator. About one-fifth of the troposphere is made up of oxygen. Nearly four-fifths is a gas called nitrogen, and the rest is made up of argon, carbon dioxide, and small amounts of other gases. The top of the troposphere is called the **tropopause.** Here, the air does not have enough oxygen for living things to survive.

Above the tropopause lies the **stratosphere.** This layer is about 21 miles (35 kilometers) thick. Its upper boundary is called the **stratopause.** The stratosphere contains a gas called **ozone,** which is related to oxygen. The ozone acts as a protective shield around Earth. Light from the sun contains powerful ultraviolet rays, which can be harmful to living things. Fortunately, the ozone layer stops most of these rays from reaching Earth.

The next layer of Earth's atmosphere is the **mesosphere,** which is about 20 miles (32 kilometers) thick. The lowest temperatures in Earth's atmosphere occur at the top of the mesosphere, called the **mesopause.**

Air pressure

The layers of the atmosphere are like blankets on a bed. If you lie under a lot of blankets, they feel heavy. The large mass of air in the atmosphere is very heavy and presses down hard on Earth. Scientists call this **air pressure.** When you stand on the seashore, you are at sea level. Here, more air is pressing down on you than anywhere else. The farther up you go from sea level, the less dense the air becomes. Its pressure becomes less and less. The **thermosphere,** the uppermost layer of Earth's atmosphere, has very little air. Its lower portion, called the **ionosphere,** reflects radio waves back to Earth. The upper portion of the thermosphere, called the **exosphere,** gradually fades into outer space more than 1,000 miles (1,600 kilometers) above Earth.

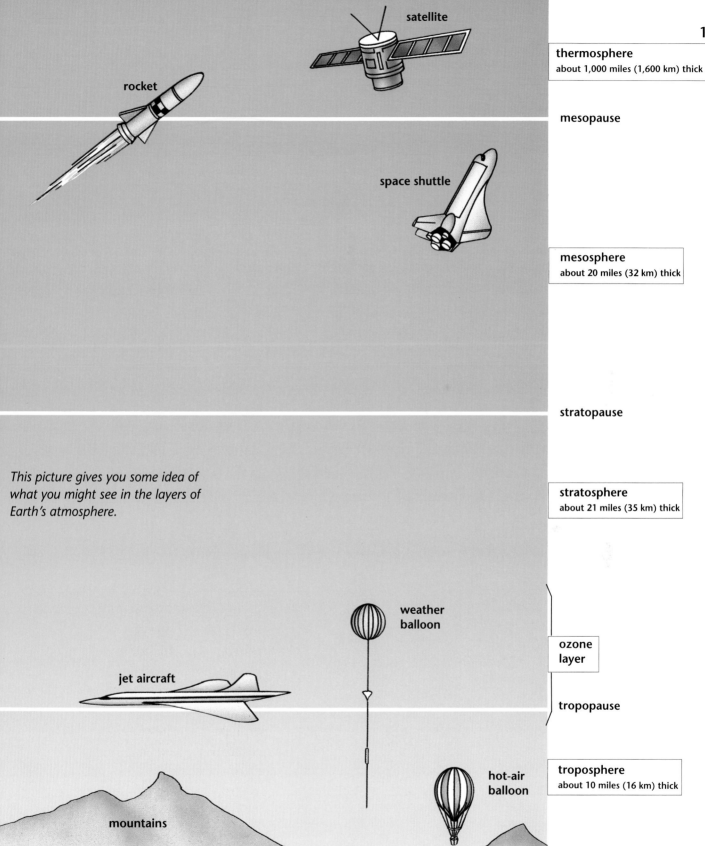

thermosphere
about 1,000 miles (1,600 km) thick

satellite

rocket

mesopause

space shuttle

mesosphere
about 20 miles (32 km) thick

stratopause

This picture gives you some idea of what you might see in the layers of Earth's atmosphere.

stratosphere
about 21 miles (35 km) thick

weather balloon

ozone layer

jet aircraft

tropopause

troposphere
about 10 miles (16 km) thick

hot-air balloon

mountains

sea level

Land on the move

Look at a map of the world. Can you see the shapes of Africa and South America? Does it look as if they will fit together? Make a jigsaw puzzle of the two shapes and find out if they do.

Moving continents

In the early 1900's, Alfred Wegener, a German scientist, studied **fossils** in rocks from Africa and South America. Fossils are imprints or remains of plants or animals usually found in rocks. He found that the fossils on both continents were the remains of the same animals and plants.

He introduced the theory that mountains in different countries might once have been joined together. The Cape Mountains in South Africa, for example, could have once been joined to mountains south of Buenos Aires, in Argentina.

Wegener believed that, over millions of years, the continents had gradually moved away from each other. They are still moving today. Scientists call this movement the **continental drift**.

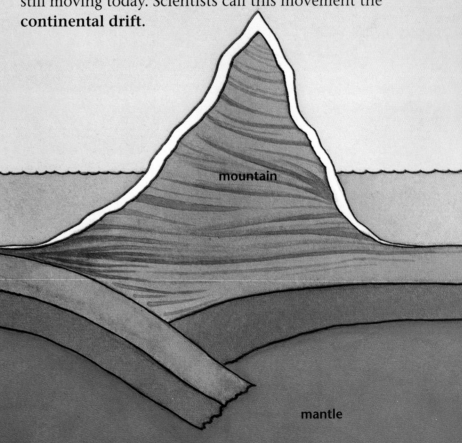

mountain

mantle

All one land

You will need:

a map of the world

a pencil

a sheet of tracing paper

a piece of thin cardboard

glue

scissors

1. Place the tracing paper over the map and trace the outlines of the continents.

2. Glue the tracing paper onto the cardboard. Cut out the shapes with scissors.

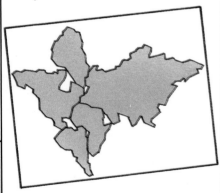

3. Now fit your jigsaw puzzle together. Do you think that the continents fit together well? Some scientists believe that the land masses of our planet once formed one huge continent called Pangaea.

Your jigsaw shapes won't fit together exactly, because the edges of the continents are under the ocean.

What are tectonic plates?

Scientists now know that Earth's crust is not formed in one huge piece, but is divided up into large sections called **tectonic plates.** The bottom part of these solid plates is made up of the mantle, the thick layer of solid rock that also contains hot, liquid rocks moving underneath Earth's crust.

What makes the plates move? It's so hot inside Earth that some of the molten rocks in the mantle are pushed upward. These liquid rocks break through the crust at its weakest points, usually where two plates meet. Then the plates are pushed apart.

In other places, cooler rocks in the mantle are pushed downwards toward the hot inner core. When the plates that make up Earth's crust are pushed together, one plate is forced below the other and melts in the mantle.

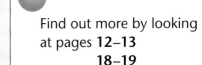
17

Find out more by looking at pages **12–13**
18–19

Hot molten rock forces the plates apart and fills the gap to form new crust.

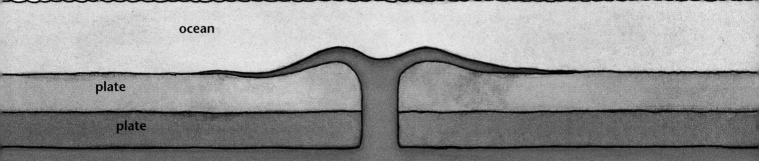

ocean

plate

plate

Find out more by looking at pages **16–17**

Making mountains

Can you believe that the top of the world's tallest mountain was once at the bottom of the ocean? Scientists discovered this surprising fact when they examined **limestone** rocks from the top of Mount Everest, which is about 5.5 miles (8.9 kilometers) above sea level. Inside these rocks, they found the remains of dead sea creatures.

Limestone is a kind of rock that is formed in layers, very slowly over thousands of years. The skeletons of animals and the remains of plants that get trapped in one of these layers are changed into **fossils**. Scientists can tell when and where different creatures lived by examining fossils.

How did rocks from the bottom of the sea get to the top of our tallest mountain? More than 60 million years ago, India was pushed up against the continent of Asia. This happened because of movements in the huge plates of Earth's crust. Before this, India and Asia were completely separate.

These rocks have been gradually pushed together to make a fold.

Mountains of the world

The mountains of the world have been formed in different ways. The Himalaya to the north of India, and the Alps to the north of Italy, were formed when plates in Earth's crust were pushed together. When rocks buckle up, or fold in this way, we call them **fold mountains.**

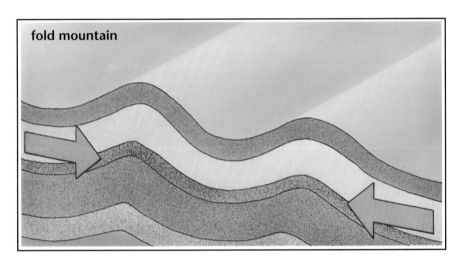

fold mountain

Another type of mountain is formed when movements of the plates inside Earth's crust create weak areas, or **faults**, in the crust. As the plates press together, the mantle pushes its way upward and cracks appear. The land between the cracks is forced up in a block-like shape. This type of mountain is called a **fault-block mountain.** The Sierra Nevada in the western United States and the mountain ranges of East Africa are examples of fault-block mountains.

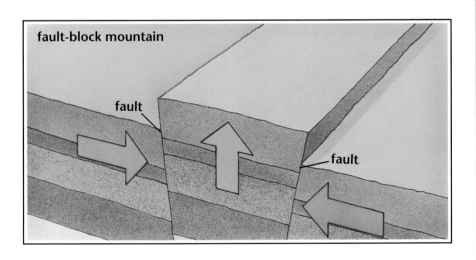

fault-block mountain

fault

fault

A paper mountain range

Rocks feel hard and solid when you touch them. But when some rocks are pushed together with great force, they can bend and fold just like a piece of paper.

See for yourself how this can happen.

You will need:

a stack of paper, at least several sheets

Think of each sheet of paper as a layer of rock.

What happens when you push the sheets of paper together? The sheets rise up into a peak. You have made a paper mountain range! In the same way, Earth's movements have made some mountains by pushing rocks together.

Find out more by looking at pages **16–17**

When Earth shakes

Would you be frightened if the ground started shaking under your feet? Sudden, violent movements under Earth's surface are called **earthquakes.** Sometimes, the ground shakes so hard that buildings fall, roads and bridges collapse, and electric power lines break.

Look at this map of the world. The black lines show the edges of the huge sections, or tectonic plates, in Earth's crust. The red areas show places where earthquakes are strongest and happen most often. Most earthquakes occur near the edges of the plates. Some of the earthquake areas, or **zones,** are on land, and some are under the sea.

*This map of the world shows that **volcanoes** and earthquakes usually occur in the same areas of the world. These areas are usually situated on the edges of the tectonic plates. You can read about volcanoes on pages 22–23.*

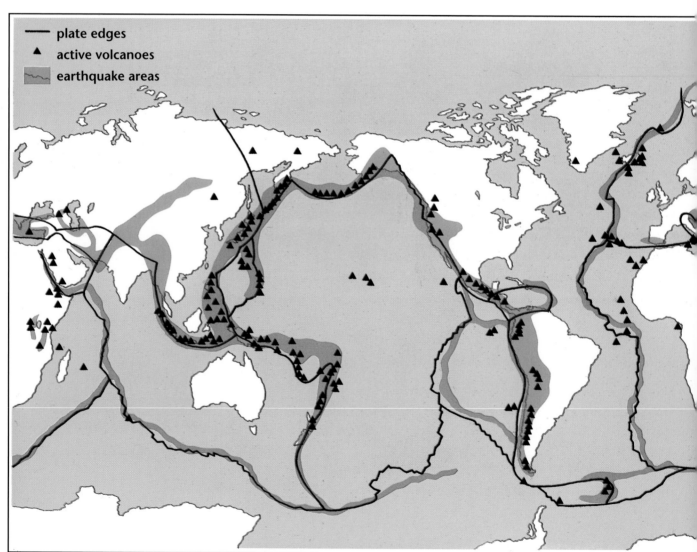

— plate edges
▲ active volcanoes
    earthquake areas

Earthquakes can cause widespread damage to homes, schools, factories, and other buildings. This house was damaged during an earthquake in the United States.

Why do earthquakes happen?

On the plates, there are cracks, or faults, in Earth's crust. Over many years, the plates slide past each other slowly, but sometimes the rocks get stuck together. Then the intense heat from inside Earth keeps pushing them until they bend. Eventually, the pressure suddenly jolts them free, sending shock waves through the ground.

Measuring earthquakes

Scientists measure earthquakes in different ways. The **Richter scale** is based on data obtained by a *seismograph*, an instrument that records ground movements. Each number on the scale of 0 to 10 represents ground motion 10 times greater than that represented by the next lower number. To measure the largest earthquakes, scientists use the **moment magnitude scale.** This is similar to the Richter scale but uses a more sensitive system for recording data. The **Mercalli scale** measures the amount of damage an earthquake causes. A score of 1 means no damage, but a score of 12 means the earthquake has destroyed whole buildings.

Giant waves

Earthquakes under the sea sometimes make giant ocean waves, called **tsunamis.** These destructive waves can be as high as 100 feet (30 meters), and happen most often in the Pacific Ocean near Japan.

steam, gas, and dust

When Earth spits fire

Suddenly, a fountain of fire bursts from underground, showering the land or sea with hot, liquid rock and clouds of dust and gas. This is what happens when a **volcano** erupts.

On our planet, there are more than 500 active volcanoes, which might erupt at any time. Only about 25 volcanoes actually erupt each year, however. Some, such as Stromboli in Italy, erupt frequently. Some volcanoes are under the surface of the ocean.

Turn to the map of the world on page 20, and look at the edges of the large sections, or plates, in Earth's crust. The red areas show where most earthquakes happen. Most volcanoes also occur near the edges of these plates.

volcanic bombs

flowing lava

layers of ash and lava

What happens inside Earth?

Underneath its surface, Earth is a mass of hot rocks and metals. In the mantle, the layer under Earth's crust, it is so hot that some rocks have melted and become molten rocks.

As the rocks melt, they produce gases. The mixture of gas and molten rock is called **magma.** Because it is mixed with bubbles of gas, the molten rock weighs less than the solid rocks around it. The magma rises toward Earth's surface and collects in hollow spaces called **chambers.** Some magma chambers are only 1.8 miles (3 kilometers) underground.

magma

A volcano erupts

Near the edges of the sections called tectonic plates, there are weak places called cracks, or **fissures**. Strong pressure underground forces the magma to carve a tunnel up through these cracks. When the magma bursts out, a volcano erupts. Gases from the magma shoot into Earth's atmosphere, and a hot, fiery liquid, called **lava**, flows over the ground.

If the lava is thin, like soup, it spreads out and forms a wide, flat volcano. Mauna Loa, on Hawaii in the Pacific Ocean, is a volcano like this. When the lava is thick, like syrup, it makes a cone-shaped volcano with steep sides, such as Mount Fuji in Japan.

23

Find out more by looking at pages **12–13**
16–17
20–21

Mount Etna is one of the world's most famous active volcanoes. It has erupted at least 260 times since its first recorded eruption in about 700 B.C.

Hot water and steam

Sometimes, underground water is heated by very hot rocks to a temperature above the boiling point. The water changes to steam. Then jets of boiling water and steam, called **geysers,** burst out of the ground. The rocks that boil the water are sometimes heated by magma chambers.

How rocks are made

Take a close look at a small rock. Can you see tiny pieces of different colors and shapes in it? These pieces are called **minerals.** Most rocks are a mixture of different minerals. For example, **granite** consists mainly of quartz and feldspar. It may also contain mica and hornblende.

Scientists who study rocks are called **geologists.** Geologists have classified all the kinds of rock into three main groups, according to how the rock was originally formed. These groups are **igneous** rock, **sedimentary** rock, and **metamorphic** rock.

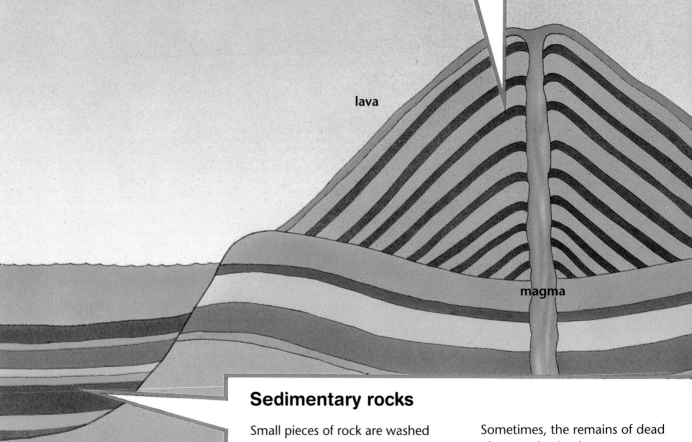

lava

magma

Igneous rocks

Molten rock that bursts from the mantle under Earth's crust cools down and becomes solid. This is called igneous rock. You can clearly see crystal shapes in some igneous rocks, such as granite and basalt. Crystals are clear solids made from atoms arranged in an orderly pattern. An atom is one of the basic units of matter.

Sedimentary rocks

Small pieces of rock are washed down into the sea. These pieces settle in layers, or strata. Over millions of years, more and more layers press down on each other and turn the bottom layers into hard, sedimentary rock.

Sometimes, the remains of dead plants and animals turn to stone in the layers of sedimentary rocks. These remains, called fossils, tell us about life on Earth long ago.

You will need:

water

some dry clay and sand

a tablespoon

a glass jar,
with a lid

Shake and settle

1. Fill the jar halfway with water, and put about four spoonfuls of clay and four spoonfuls of sand in it.

2. Screw the lid on tightly and shake the jar. Watch the clay and sand settle. The particles of sand are more dense, so they settle first at the bottom of the jar. Then the smaller, lighter clay particles form layers (according to their sizes) above the layer of sand.

Imagine this happening under the ocean for millions of years. Eventually, the weight of the top layers presses the lower layers into hard, sedimentary rock.

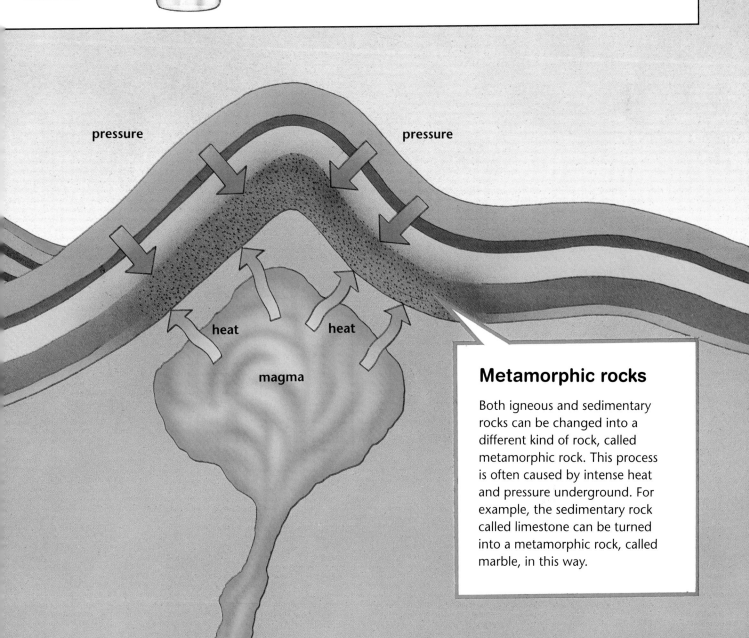

pressure

pressure

heat

heat

magma

Metamorphic rocks

Both igneous and sedimentary rocks can be changed into a different kind of rock, called metamorphic rock. This process is often caused by intense heat and pressure underground. For example, the sedimentary rock called limestone can be turned into a metamorphic rock, called marble, in this way.

Find out more by looking at pages **12–13**

What lies under the oceans?

Nearly three-fourths of Earth's surface is covered by water. The land under the oceans is made up of mountains, valleys and large, flat plains, just like the land on the continents. It even has volcanoes!

The water in the oceans

Where did the oceans come from? Some scientists believe that the oceans were formed about 4 billion years ago. At this time, hot rocks inside Earth cooled down and water vapor in the air fell as rain. The rain gradually filled the low places in Earth's crust and formed the first oceans.

The **continental shelf** is the real edge of the continent, where the land slopes away to meet the ocean floor. It lies about 600 feet (180 meters) below sea level.

Ocean ridges are mountain ranges on the ocean floor where molten rock has pushed its way up from beneath Earth's crust.

Away from the shelf, the ocean floor drops sharply to about 18,000 feet (5,000 meters) below sea level. The deep ocean bottom is known as the **abyss**.

At the bottom of the sea

How do we know what lies at the bottom of the ocean? Scientists who study the ocean are called **oceanographers.** With the help of very accurate instruments, they have made maps of the ocean floor.

Modern oceanographers use a device called an **echo sounder** to measure the depth of an ocean. An echo sounder sends sound waves down to the ocean floor, and measures how long it takes for them to echo back to the surface of the water. The longer the echo takes to return, the greater the depth.

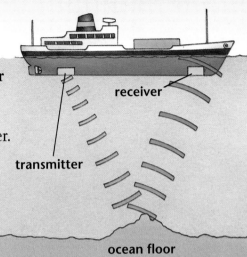

A transmitter on board an echo-sounding ship sends sound signals to the bottom of the sea. The receiver measures the time it takes for the signals to return.

receiver

transmitter

ocean floor

Volcanoes can erupt at ocean ridges and trenches. Sometimes they erupt above sea level, making volcanic islands. The islands of Hawaii are volcanic islands.

A **trench** is a long, narrow valley in the ocean floor. The world's deepest trench is the Mariana Trench, in the western part of the Pacific Ocean. It is over 6 miles (9.5 kilometers) deep.

Why does the ocean move?

The waters of the ocean are moving all the time. The surface of the water moves up and down as **waves** travel across the surface. The level of the ocean rises and falls with the **tides**. What makes these movements that we call waves and tides? Waves are caused by winds, earthquakes, and the gravitational pull of the sun and moon. Waves move forward, but under each wave, the water moves around in a circle. As each wave reaches the shore, it causes the water near the shore to break into surf.

Water on the surface of the ocean moves up and down while the waves travel along its surface. The water does not really move forward until the wave reaches the shore.

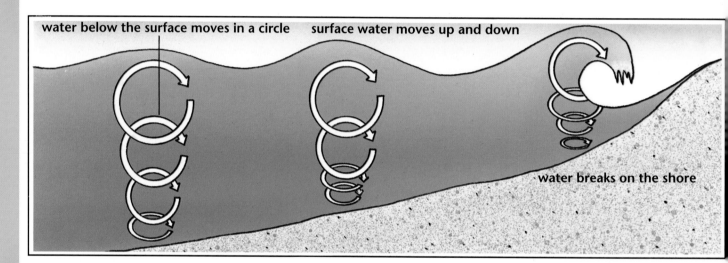

water below the surface moves in a circle   surface water moves up and down

water breaks on the shore

You will need:

a thin rope, around 13 feet (4 meters) long

a tree or post

Making waves

1. Tie one end of the rope to a tree or post, at the same height as your waist. Hold the other end and stand about 10 feet (3 meters) away.

2. Move the rope quickly up and down. A wave moves along the rope, but the rope itself does not move forward.

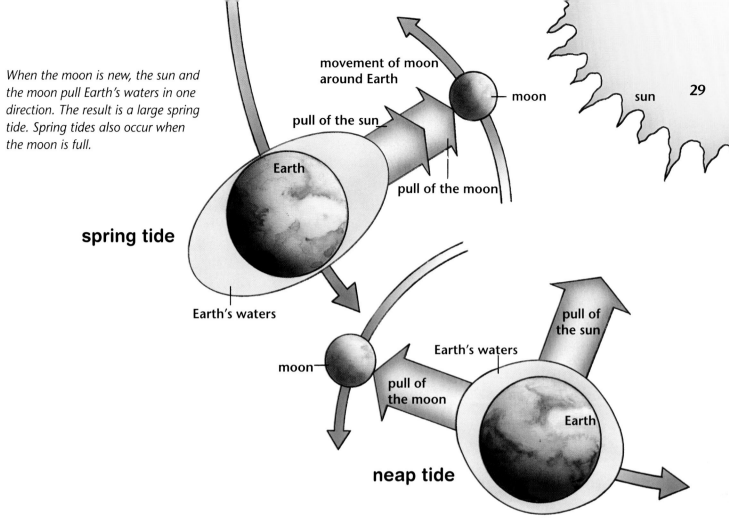

When the moon is new, the sun and the moon pull Earth's waters in one direction. The result is a large spring tide. Spring tides also occur when the moon is full.

movement of moon around Earth

pull of the sun

moon

sun

Earth

pull of the moon

spring tide

Earth's waters

moon

Earth's waters

pull of the sun

pull of the moon

neap tide

Earth

When the moon is halfway between new and full, the pull of the sun is at right angles to the pull of the moon. The result is a small neap tide.

High tide and low tide

Have you ever gone to a beach along the coast to walk or play, but found it completely covered by water? Sometimes, you have to wait as long as six hours before the seashore is uncovered again! These changes in the level of water are called tides. **High tide** is when the water covers the shore. **Low tide** is when the beach is uncovered again. There are one or two high and low tides each day.

Tides happen because of a force called **gravity.** The gravity of the moon pulls Earth's waters toward the moon. And the gravity of the sun pulls Earth's waters toward the sun.

The moon takes about one month to move around Earth. When the moon is either new or full, the sun, moon, and Earth lie in a straight line. The tides that happen then are called **spring tides**, occurring about twice each month. During spring tides, the difference between the level of water at high tide and at low tide is very large. When the sun, moon, and Earth are at right angles to each other, the tides are called **neap tides**, also occurring about twice each month. This is when the difference between high tide and low tide is very small.

The shape of the coast

The difference between the level of water at high tide and low tide also varies with the shape of the coast. On the coasts of the Mediterranean Sea, the difference may be as little as 1 foot (30 centimeters). In the Bay of Fundy in eastern Canada, the difference may be as much as 40 feet (12 meters).

30

Find out more by looking at
pages **24–25**
        34–35

Wearing rocks away

Have you ever seen waves pounding against the coastline? The force of the water moves the sand and pebbles on the beach. Water from oceans and rivers is always moving sand, soil, and rocks from one place to another. This process is called **erosion**. Wind and ice also wear away, or **erode**, rocks and soil. Over thousands of years, erosion can move mountains, dig out or fill in valleys, and change the direction of rivers.

Rocks feel hard and solid. But they can be broken down. For example, water that seeps into cracks in rocks may freeze and expand into ice. The ice splits the rock and breaks it into smaller pieces. These pieces may be washed away by oceans and rivers, blown away by the wind, or moved down a mountainside by a frozen river of ice called a **glacier.**

Over millions of years, loose stones carried along by large, fast-flowing rivers can erode a passage through solid rock. The huge valleys this process makes are called **canyons**. In Arizona, the Colorado River has carved out a deep canyon called the Grand Canyon.

Chemicals in water can dissolve some rocks, leaving behind large caves. Rain water often mixes with carbon dioxide gas, making a weak acid that eats away some types of rock.

Parts of the Grand Canyon in Arizona are almost 18 miles (30 kilometers) wide and 1 mile (1.6 kilometers) deep. The different layers of red and brown rock look especially brilliant at sunset.

How do rocks change?

In the Arches National Park in Utah, the center of this rock has been worn away to form a large, arched opening.

Have you ever seen an archway of rock jutting out into the sea? The moving water has worn a hole through the weaker middle parts of this rock. You might see a rock arch inland, too. Strong winds blow sand against the rock, wearing away the weaker parts but leaving the firm parts still standing.

Small pieces of rock that are washed or blown away form **sediment**. The sediment will settle somewhere else in layers. Eventually, these layers are pressed together to make new rocks, called **sedimentary rocks.**

Flowing river water washes sand, clay, and soil down toward the sea. In some places, where a river meets the sea, this sediment piles up in layers that form a piece of new land called a **delta.**

Icebreaker ships cut a path through the thick Antarctic ice, so that other ships can travel past.

When ice covers Earth

Have you ever made a snowball? Snow is soft and fluffy when it falls from the sky, but when you press it into a ball, it can become quite hard. If you press it very tightly, it turns into a lump of ice.

And it is so cold at the North and South poles that the snow there never has a chance to melt. This happens in nature, too. When snow first falls, it is light and soft and melts easily. But as more snow falls, it presses down into tightly packed layers, which then turn to ice.

Sheets of ice

Some areas of Earth are covered by huge sheets of ice and snow all year. Around the North Pole, there is no land, but an **ice sheet** covers the Arctic Ocean. An ice sheet also covers most of Greenland and some northern parts of Canada and Europe. The largest ice sheet in the world lies around the South Pole. It covers about 5,400,000 square miles (14,000,000 square kilometers) of the huge continent called Antarctica. This ice sheet has an average thickness of about 7,100 feet (2,200 meters). The Antarctic ice contains about three-fourths of Earth's fresh water.

Our frozen past

For hundreds of years, many layers of ice have been forming in the Arctic and in Antarctica. Scientists can dig down into the ice to find traces of the past. In Antarctica, they have found fossils of plant life, coal, and other minerals.

Ice taken from deep down under the surface of Greenland shows that the air has been polluted with lead for hundreds of years. Samples of ice also prove that lead pollution has become much worse during the past 100 years. Scientists believe that most of this pollution is caused by the lead in gasoline.

What is an ice age?

The huge ice sheets around the North and South Poles were once even bigger than they are now. In the past, there were long periods of time when ice covered large areas of North America and northern Europe. These periods are called **ice ages.**

ocean
ice
land

This map shows which areas of the world were covered with ice during the Pleistocene Ice Age.

The most recent ice age began about 2 million years ago and ended about 11,500 years ago. It is known as the Pleistocene Ice Age. During each ice age, the ice sheets advance and retreat several times.

An ice age generally lasts about 100,000 years. Between ice ages, there are **interglacial periods** lasting from 10,000 to 20,000 years, when the ice melts and retreats.

Why do ice ages happen?

Most scientists believe that ice ages are caused by a regular change in the shape of Earth's orbit around the sun. This change seems to happen periodically, and makes the surface of the planet cool and causes huge ice sheets to form. Since the last ice retreat began less than 20,000 years ago, we are now living in an interglacial period. And some time in the future, the ice will advance again.

Valley glaciers and icebergs

In mountainous regions, a river of ice may flow down a valley. This is called a **valley glacier.** A glacier can move at different speeds, from a few inches (centimeters) a year to as much as 660 feet (200 meters) a year.

What is a valley glacier?

Glaciers begin in small dips or hollows on mountainsides. Every year more snow falls into these hollows than melts. The weight of the snow eventually squeezes the air out of the bottom layers of the snow to form ice. Where this ice meets the rock below, pressure generates energy to melt the ice.

The melted water on the rock surface seeps into tiny cracks in the rock. The water then freezes and expands, forcing the cracks open, allowing more water to seep in and freeze. Finally, a piece of rock breaks off. This process is called **freeze-thaw.**

In the hollow, the freeze-thaw causes more pieces of rock to break away, making the hollow bigger. The hollow is now called a **cirque.**

Moving ice

When the layer of ice becomes very heavy, it starts to flow out of the hollow and down the valley. It is now a glacier. As it moves downhill, the glacier picks up tons of sand, gravel, and broken rock. These materials are deposited along the way or pushed ahead of the glacier, forming uneven ridges called **moraines.**

Eventually, the glacier reaches the lowlands, where the air is warm enough for the ice to melt.

The long, narrow rivers of ice that flow down mountain valleys are called valley glaciers.

Find out more by looking at pages **32–33**

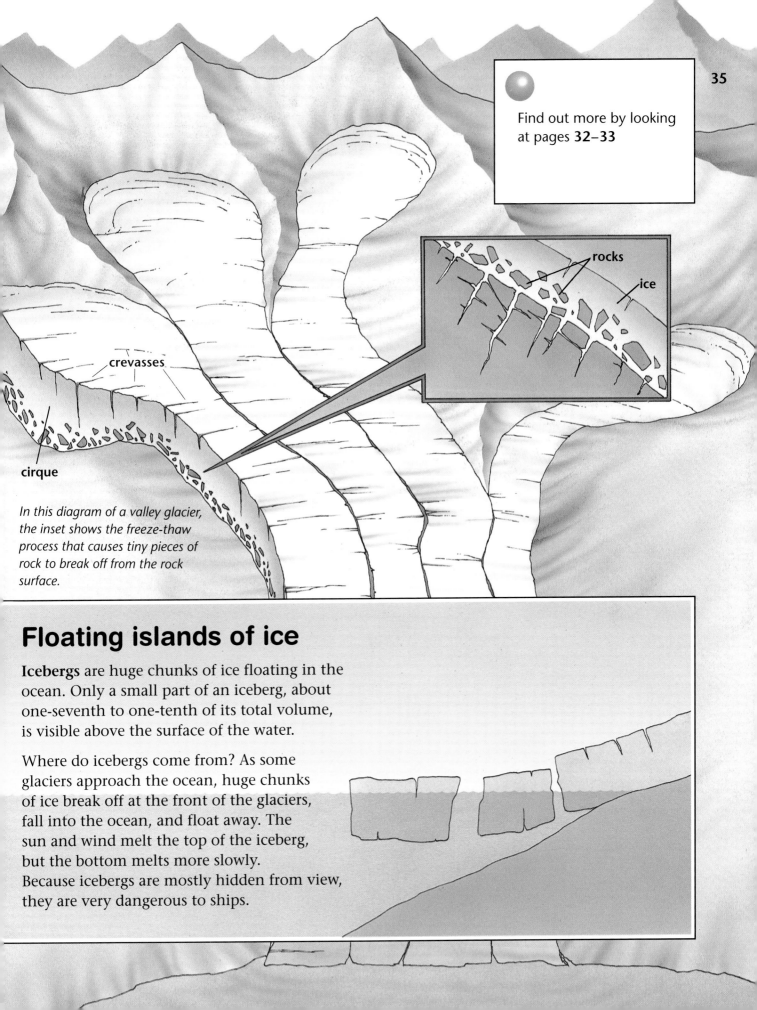

rocks

ice

crevasses

cirque

In this diagram of a valley glacier, the inset shows the freeze-thaw process that causes tiny pieces of rock to break off from the rock surface.

Floating islands of ice

Icebergs are huge chunks of ice floating in the ocean. Only a small part of an iceberg, about one-seventh to one-tenth of its total volume, is visible above the surface of the water.

Where do icebergs come from? As some glaciers approach the ocean, huge chunks of ice break off at the front of the glaciers, fall into the ocean, and float away. The sun and wind melt the top of the iceberg, but the bottom melts more slowly. Because icebergs are mostly hidden from view, they are very dangerous to ships.

Days and seasons

In most places on Earth, the sky darkens and then becomes light again in regular periods of time we call days and nights. Do you know why?

Another regular period of time is called a year. A year lasts for about 365 days. But how do you know that a year has passed if you don't have a calendar to help you count the days? One way we can tell a year is passing is by the way the amount of daylight varies at different times of the year. Let's find out how this happens.

The spinning Earth

Think of Earth as an orange with a knitting needle stuck through the middle from the North Pole to the South Pole. This needle is like the axle that a wheel spins on. Earth turns on this imaginary axle, or **axis**. Each complete turn, or **rotation**, takes 24 hours.

Daylight comes from the sun. The parts of Earth that face the sun are lit up. The parts of Earth that face away from the sun are dark.

How many seasons?

Earth is not only **rotating** on its axis, it is also **revolving** around the sun. It takes about 365 days for our planet to make a complete **revolution** around the sun. We call this period of time a year.

During the year, different parts of Earth's surface face the sun for longer or for shorter periods. In most parts of the world, people have divided the year into four periods, known as **seasons:** spring, summer, autumn, and winter. During the summer season, there is more daylight. In winter, there is less. In spring and autumn, the hours of light and dark are about the same. People in some parts of the world divide their year into only two seasons, because the amount of daylight they receive does not vary so much. But one season may be rainy and the other dry, as in some parts of the tropics.

Earth's axis is not at right angles to the sun. It is slightly tilted. This means that each of the poles is tilted away from the sun for half the year, and is therefore in the dark. For the other half of the year, each pole is tilted toward the sun and is therefore bathed in sunlight, even at midnight. So the two polar regions have one dark and one sunny season.

We call the period of time it takes for Earth to revolve, or orbit, around the sun a year.

Earth rotates on its axis once every 24 hours.

Earth's axis

In December, the South Pole is tilted toward the sun. Places in the southern half of Earth are enjoying summer, with more than 12 hours of daylight. At the same time, it is winter in the northern half of Earth.

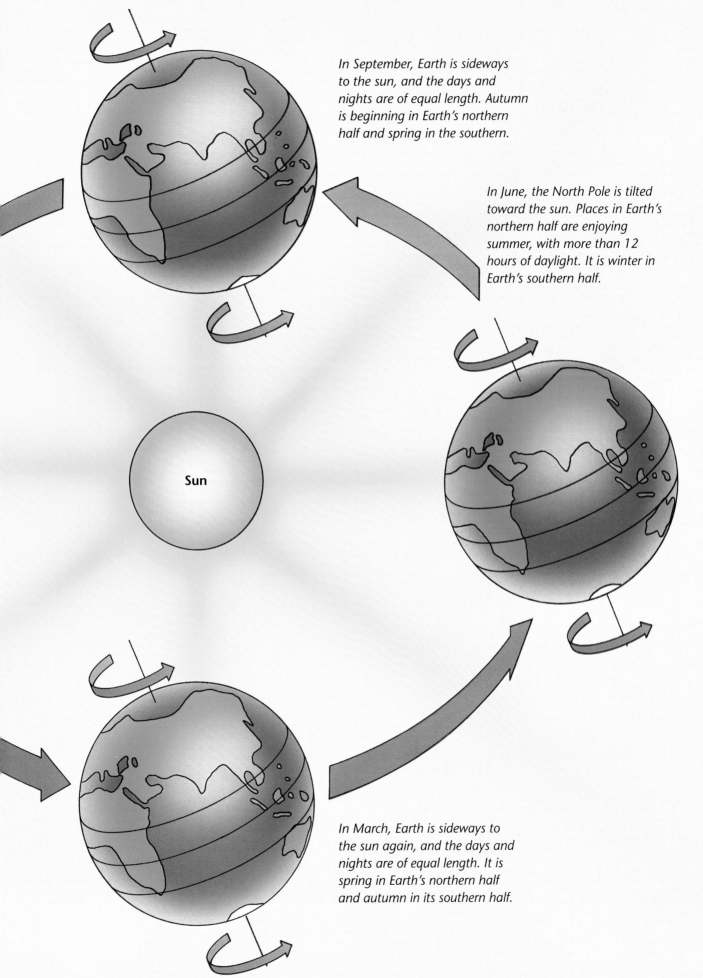

In September, Earth is sideways to the sun, and the days and nights are of equal length. Autumn is beginning in Earth's northern half and spring in the southern.

In June, the North Pole is tilted toward the sun. Places in Earth's northern half are enjoying summer, with more than 12 hours of daylight. It is winter in Earth's southern half.

Sun

In March, Earth is sideways to the sun again, and the days and nights are of equal length. It is spring in Earth's northern half and autumn in its southern half.

Find out more by looking at pages **14–15**

What is the weather?

What is your weather like today? Is it sunny, cold, wet, or dry? What causes these different kinds of weather? Heat and light from the sun travel through Earth's atmosphere. The sun's rays affect the air in four ways. They can change its **temperature**, or the amount of heat it contains. They can change its humidity, or the amount of water it contains. They can change the **air pressure**, or the force of the atmosphere pushing on Earth. And they can change the **wind**, or the way the air moves.

Temperature

Most of the heat given off by the sun is lost in space. About one-third of the sunlight that does reach the atmosphere is reflected back into space by the clouds. Less than half the sunlight that gets to Earth's atmosphere actually reaches the planet's surface. This sunlight warms the ground, oceans, and lakes, which then reflect warmth back into the air.

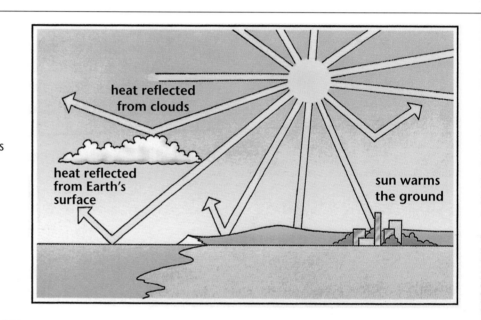

Humidity

Humidity is the amount of water vapor in the air. When sunlight warms oceans, lakes, and rivers, some of the water turns into water vapor. The vapor rises into the air, condenses, and forms tiny drops of water that float in the air as clouds. These drops fall to Earth as **precipitation.** That's what scientists call rain, snow, hail, or sleet.

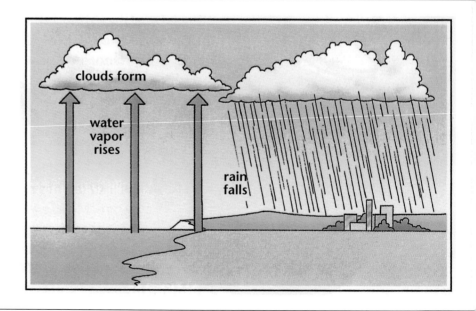

Air pressure

What difference does the weight of the air make? Warm air weighs less than cool air, which is why hot-air balloons stay up in the sky. Lighter weights put less pressure on whatever is underneath them. So where the air is warmer, the air pressure is lower. Cool air weighs more, so where the air is cooler, the air pressure is higher.

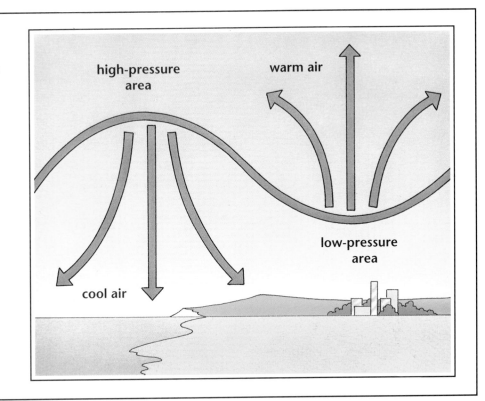

Wind

What is the wind? The wind is air moving from one place to another. Air always moves from where the pressure is high to where the pressure is low. The greater the difference between the levels of high pressure and low pressure, the stronger the wind movement.

Which way does the north wind blow? It blows from the north toward the south. Winds are always named after the direction from which they blow.

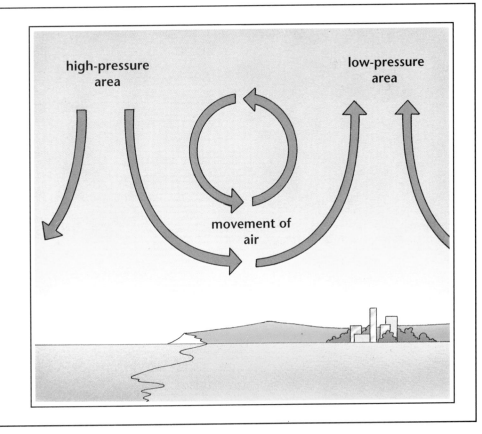

Find out more by looking at pages **38–39**

Predicting the weather

When you're planning a picnic with your friends, you need to know that the weather will be good, so that you can enjoy yourselves outside. Many people need to know what the weather will be like so that they can plan their work or other outdoor activities.

Scientists who study the weather are called **meteorologists**. They use many different instruments to collect information about temperature, air pressure, wind speed, and direction. They also study the amount of moisture in the air.

How much moisture is there in the air?

You will need:

a pencil

a ruler

a piece of thin cardboard, 6 inches × 1.5 inches (15 centimeters × 4 centimeters)

a piece of stiff cardboard, 8.5 inches × 11 inches (21 centimeters × 27.5 centimeters)

a pair of scissors

tape

a strand of hair, about 8 inches (20 centimeters) long

a piece of wood, 11 inches × 2 inches × 2 inches (27.5 centimeters × 5 centimeters × 5 centimeters)

six thumbtacks

a colored pen with a fine point

You can make your own hygrometer. Keep a chart of your results every day for three weeks. Can you forecast whether it will be wet or dry during the fourth week?

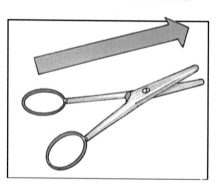

1. Using the ruler, draw an arrow about 5 inches by 1 inch (12.5 centimeters × 2.5 centimeters) on the thin cardboard. Cut out the arrow.

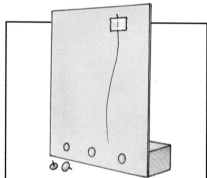

3. Using thumb tacks, attach the stiff cardboard to the long edge of the piece of wood.

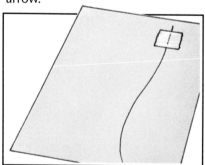

2. Tape one end of the strand of hair to the center-top of the stiff cardboard.

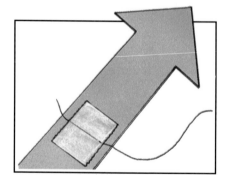

4. Attach the free end of the hair to the middle of the back of the arrow.

Instruments for forecasting

Meteorologists measure the speed of the wind with an **anemometer** and the amount of moisture with a **hygrometer.** These instruments are used in weather stations on the ground, or in aircraft, ships, and weather balloons. Meteorologists use the information from these instruments to forecast the weather.

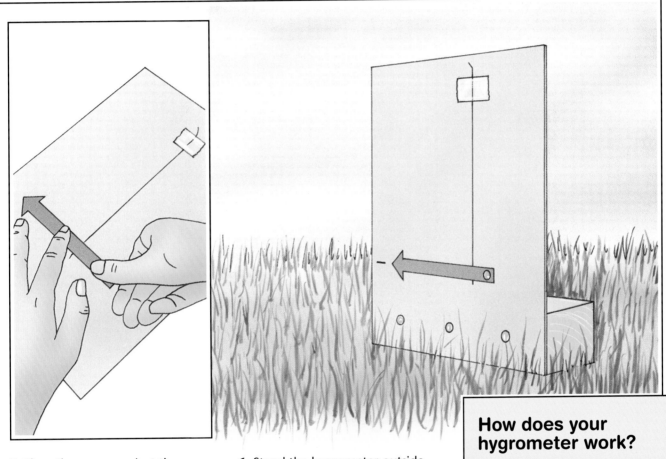

5. Place the arrow against the cardboard and move it until the hair is stretched out fully and also parallel to the long side of the cardboard. Then attach the end of the arrow (opposite the arrowhead) to the cardboard with a thumb tack.

6. Stand the hygrometer outside. Make sure that it can't fall over. When the sun is shining, mark on the cardboard where the arrow is pointing. Write "dry" by the side of this mark. When the weather is damp, the arrow will point lower. Mark its new position and write "damp" on the cardboard.

How does your hygrometer work?

On a damp day, the strand of hair will absorb moisture from the air. This will make the hair stretch and so the arrow points lower. On dry, sunny days, the hair dries out and becomes shorter.

Find out more by looking
at pages **14–15**
36–37
38–39

42

What is a climate?

The weather where you live may be sunny one day and cloudy the next, or dry during one season and wet during another. Over several years, there's a pattern to these daily and seasonal changes in the weather, wherever you live. This pattern of weather over a period of time is called a **climate**.

Scientists who study climates are called **climatologists**. They say that the climate varies according to three things—the way the sun's rays reach Earth, the amount of land and sea nearby, and the height of the land above sea level.

Earth is marked into horizontal sections by imaginary lines called **lines of latitude**. A main line around the middle is called the **equator**. Two lines of latitude north of the equator are special, and they are called the Tropic of Cancer and the Arctic Circle. Two lines of latitude south of the equator are the Tropic of Capricorn and the Antarctic Circle.

The sun's rays

Near the equator, Earth's tilt causes the sun's rays to shine more directly. The direct sunlight provides enough energy to heat up land and water. In the polar regions, an equal amount of the sun's rays is spread over a wider area because the rays meet Earth's surface at more of an angle. The angle of the tilted Earth causes the rays to pass through more atmosphere at polar regions, losing heat along the way.

You can see that the sun's rays are more concentrated at the equator than anywhere else on Earth. So the countries near the equator are the hottest in the world.

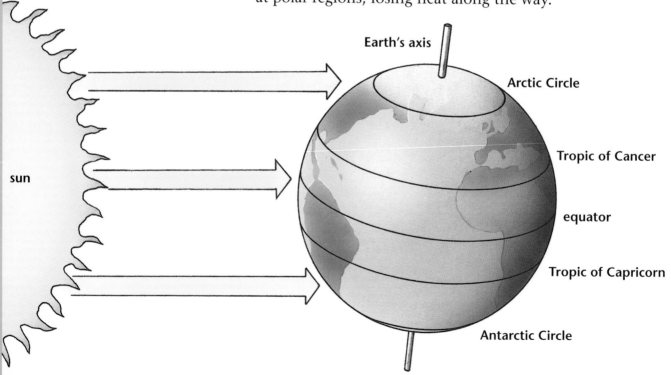

What kind of climate?

Energy from the sun warms the ground, and some of this heat is reflected back into the air. Warm air rises, and as it rises, it cools down. Places that are high above sea level, such as mountains, have cooler climates than places lower down.

Energy from the sun warms the oceans, rivers, and lakes, turning some of the water into vapor. This vapor rises to form clouds and then falls back to the ground as rain, sleet, hail, or snow. Places near the coast have wetter climates than places inland.

In tropical regions of the world, heavy rainfall can occur during the hot seasons. In India and many other countries, this heavy rain can cause flooding.

How the sun shines

You will need:

a small ball

a flashlight

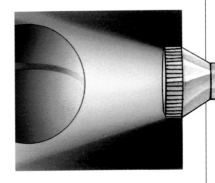

1. Hold the ball in one hand. Shine the flashlight directly onto the middle of the ball. The light at the center of the ball is similar to the sun's rays shining at the equator.

2. Now look at how the light is shining at the top of the ball. It is spread over a much wider area. This gives you an idea of how the sun shines in the polar regions.

Stormy weather

Dark clouds fill the sky and heavy rain pours down. Lightning flashes brightly and noisy thunder crashes. Do you know what causes these stormy sights and sounds?

What makes the clouds?

Heat from the sun turns water from oceans and rivers into water vapor. Movements in the air, called **convection currents**, push the vapor up in the air. Here it condenses and turns back into tiny drops of water. **Condensation** is the process by which a gas changes into a liquid.

The air is full of tiny particles of dust. A drop of water will collect around a dust particle. Clouds form where millions of these tiny drops of water gather. Thunderclouds are the biggest clouds of all. Some are as tall as 11 miles (18 kilometers) from top to bottom.

Lightning

During a storm, strong winds blow the tiny particles of dust and water around inside the cloud and make them collide with one another. Normally, each particle in the cloud has a positive and a negative electrical charge. But when the particles collide with each other, these charges separate. Most of the positively charged particles move to the top of the cloud, and most of the negatively charged particles move to the bottom.

Lightning is a giant spark of electricity in the sky. The spark happens when the negative charges in a thundercloud meet the positive charges in another cloud, or on the ground. Lightning strikes somewhere about 100 times every second!

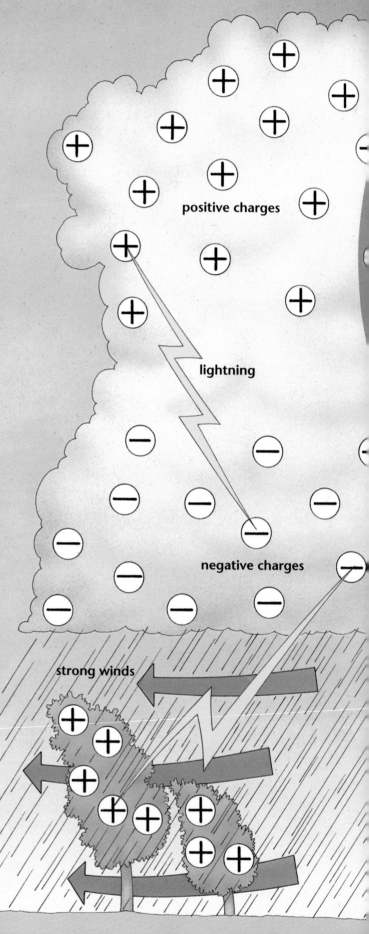

positive charges

lightning

negative charges

strong winds

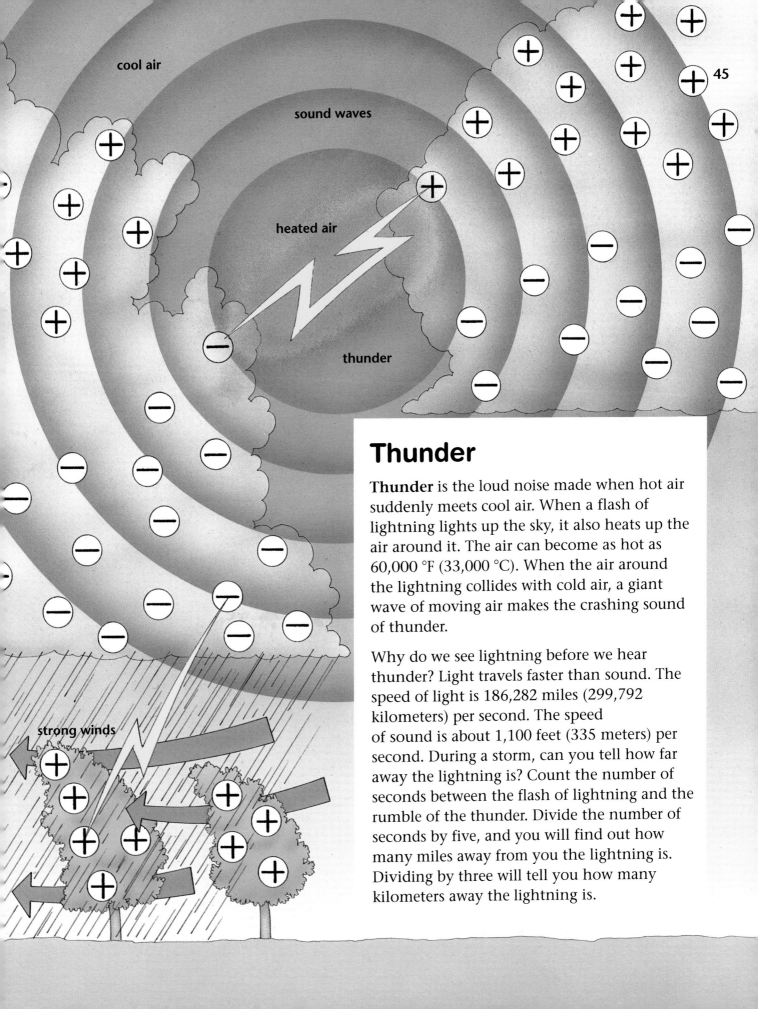

cool air

sound waves

heated air

thunder

strong winds

Thunder

Thunder is the loud noise made when hot air suddenly meets cool air. When a flash of lightning lights up the sky, it also heats up the air around it. The air can become as hot as 60,000 °F (33,000 °C). When the air around the lightning collides with cold air, a giant wave of moving air makes the crashing sound of thunder.

Why do we see lightning before we hear thunder? Light travels faster than sound. The speed of light is 186,282 miles (299,792 kilometers) per second. The speed of sound is about 1,100 feet (335 meters) per second. During a storm, can you tell how far away the lightning is? Count the number of seconds between the flash of lightning and the rumble of the thunder. Divide the number of seconds by five, and you will find out how many miles away from you the lightning is. Dividing by three will tell you how many kilometers away the lightning is.

Dangerous weather

The weather can sometimes be very dangerous. Violent storms can create fierce, twisting winds that seriously damage anything that gets in their way.

What is a tornado?

A **tornado** is a powerful, twisting windstorm. Most tornadoes develop along a boundary, called a **front**, where cool, dry air meets warm, humid air. Large thunderclouds appear, thunder begins to rumble, and a nearby cloud becomes dark and dense.

If the warm air rises very quickly, more warm air rushes in to replace it. As this air rises, it sometimes starts to rotate. The rotating air forms a tornado which is shaped like a long, thin funnel stretching down from the cloud toward the ground. Another name for a tornado is "twister."

If this funnel meets the ground, it sucks things up like an enormous vacuum cleaner, making a swirling mass of dust and dirt, and destroying almost everything in its path.

Tornadoes can even make a house explode! When the tornado sucks up air from around the outside of the house, it makes the air pressure outside lower than the air pressure inside. The greater force of the air inside pushes the walls apart and the house explodes.

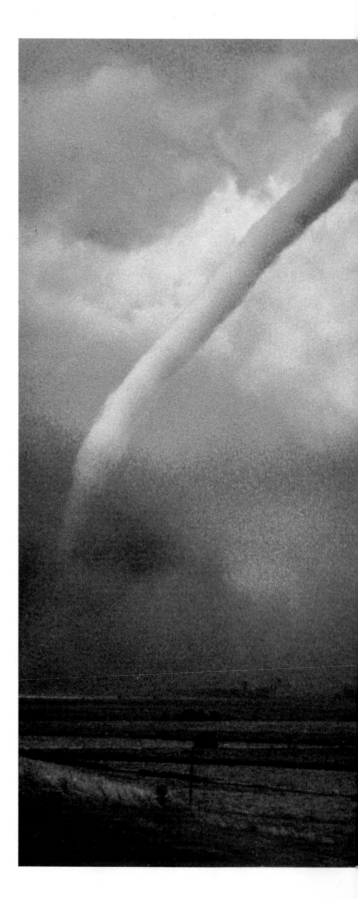

This tornado's long, narrow funnel of dust and dirt stretches from the clouds down to the ground.

The power of hurricanes

A **hurricane** is a powerful, whirling storm that forms over tropical oceans. Hurricanes can also be called typhoons or cyclones.

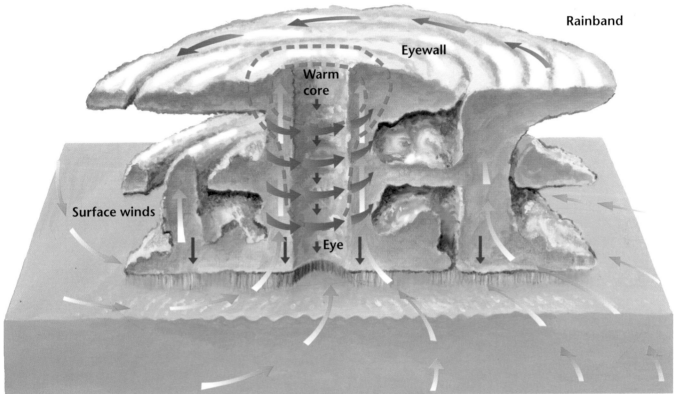

Rainband

Eyewall

Warm core

Surface winds

Eye

If you could slice through a hurricane, this is how it would look. It consists of a huge mass of wind and rain, swirling at enormous speed around a still point in the middle, called the eye. A hurricane moves forward as it rotates, creating huge, destructive waves in its path.

In tropical regions, warm air rises quickly above the ocean. It contains large amounts of water vapor that has evaporated from the ocean below. Above the ocean, the water vapor cools, turns back into water droplets, and forms storm clouds. Sometimes, the very moist air traveling upward meets strong winds that pull it up even higher. More moist air then rises from above the ocean, making a huge, swirling ring of wind and rain.

Hurricane winds rotate at speeds of up to 150 miles (240 kilometers) an hour around a calm area in the center, called the **eye** of the storm. The hurricane may last several days, moving forward at about 12 miles (20 kilometers) an hour. Most of the damage caused by hurricanes happens because the storm creates huge waves that flood the land.

This kind of storm needs a constant supply of moist air rising from warm seas. So once they reach dry land, hurricanes die out.

Water evaporates in the hot sun at these salt pans in Brazil. People can then collect the salt that is left behind.

Salt and the sea

Have you ever accidentally swallowed some water while swimming in the ocean? It probably made you gag and cough. Seawater contains a lot of salt and this makes it very unpleasant to taste, as well as unhealthy to drink.

If you were to drink salt water, you would become thirsty. Do you know why? You already have lots of salt in your body—everybody has! If you take in even more, you would feel the need to drink some liquid to water down, or **dilute,** the extra salt.

We can use both the water and the salt in the ocean, but we need to separate them first.

Collecting salt

Ninety-seven percent of the world's water is found in the salty oceans and seas. In some hot, dry countries, people collect salt from the ocean. Seawater is pumped into shallow ponds, called **salt pans.** The hot sunshine **evaporates** it, or turns the water into vapor, leaving behind salt crystals.

Human beings need to eat some salt to stay healthy. Other animals also need salt, so farmers put out blocks of this important mineral for cattle to lick. In manufacturing, salt is used mostly to produce chemicals for making materials such as glass, paper, and plastics.

Making fresh water

People in some countries in the world are so short of fresh water that they are even thinking about towing icebergs from Arctic regions to their own dry lands! Only about 3 percent of Earth's water is fresh. About three-fourths of Earth's fresh water is frozen in icecaps and other glaciers.

Fresh water can be made by taking salt out of seawater. This process is called **desalination.** The most common method of desalination is called **multistage flash distillation.** In multistage flash distillation, preheated seawater flows into a large chamber where the pressure is low. The low pressure causes some of the water to **flash**—turn quickly—into steam. The steam is condensed into salt-free water.

In multistage flash distillation, seawater passes through several distillation chambers. Each of the chambers has a lower pressure than the previous chamber.

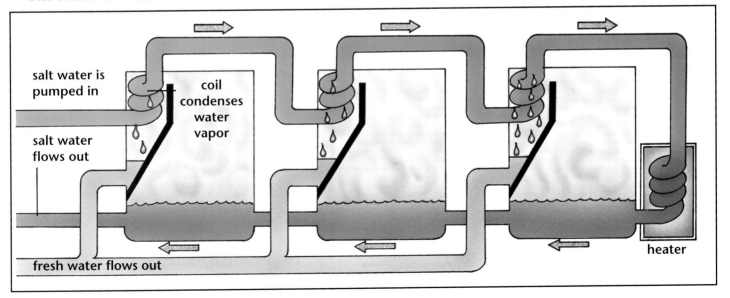

salt water is pumped in

coil condenses water vapor

salt water flows out

heater

fresh water flows out

Resources from the ocean

Have you ever gone swimming in fresh water? It isn't as easy as swimming in the ocean, because the salt in seawater helps swimmers stay afloat. Oceans are salty because as rivers flow over rocks toward the ocean, many minerals, called **salts**, dissolve in the water. In this way, millions of tons of **gold salts** and **silver salts** have been dissolved in the sea.

Much of the world's supply of **magnesium** is taken out, or extracted, directly from seawater. Magnesium is mixed with **aluminum** to make light metals. **Bromine** is also extracted from seawater and used to manufacture medicines, as well as photographic film.

Food from the ocean

The ocean provides us with food. During the early 1990's, the worldwide fish catch totaled about 108 million tons (98 million metric tons) each year. Some kinds of algae, such as nori, are also good to eat. Other algae provide chemicals, called **alginates**, that are used to make sausages and paper.

These fishermen are pulling nets back on-board their fishing boat.

Mining the ocean floor

Deep down on the ocean floor, there are fist-sized lumps, or **nodules**, that contain lots of minerals. The nodules are made up of layers, like an onion. They are found in areas where many sea creatures live. The sea creatures absorb and store minerals in their bodies. When they die and sink to the bottom of the sea, the minerals in their bodies are left in the mud after their bodies have decomposed.

These nodules usually contain **iron** and **manganese**, which are used to make hard steel for tools. Some nodules contain valuable minerals like **cobalt**, **nickel**, and **copper**.

It is more difficult and expensive to extract minerals from the ocean than from the ground. But the reserves of minerals on land are being used up quickly. So one day soon, we may need to use the ocean's resources.

Scientists are exploring the possibility of building special machines to mine the nodules on the ocean floor. These machines would probably work by remote control.

Special machines like giant vacuum cleaners may be used to mine the seabed, sucking up nodules that contain valuable minerals.

Resources from Earth's crust

Everything on Earth is made up of a combination of building blocks called the **chemical elements.** There are 109 recognized elements; 91 occur naturally on Earth. Many of these are metals. Most metals can combine with other chemical elements to form **compounds.** These compounds are called **minerals** when they are found in rocks and soil.

How are metals formed?

Most minerals grow in liquids, sometimes forming where molten rocks from beneath Earth's crust cool and harden. These metal-containing rocks are called **ores.** The large iron ore deposits in Kiruna, in northern Sweden, were formed in this way.

As the molten rocks cool, a mixture of minerals, gas, and hot water forces its way into cracks in the rocks. This mixture also cools and hardens to form thin lines that are rich in metallic minerals like **lead, copper,** and **zinc.**

Some metal elements do not combine easily with other elements. These metals, like **gold, silver,** and **platinum,** occur naturally in Earth's crust as small grains, or as larger lumps of metal. Falling rain and rivers wash these metals out of rocks on Earth's surface. The heavier metals drop in one area and form **placer deposits.**

When these deposits occur on river beds, special dredgers sort the metals from gravel deposits. Powerful water jets are used to break up dry placer deposits. The gravel is washed and separated from the metal ore.

The layer of iron ore is visible in this rock from an open-cast iron ore mine.

This enormous open-cast iron ore mine is situated at Mount Whaleback in western Australia.

Special machines drill into the rock surfaces in underground iron ore mines.

Mining

Mining for metals can take place on Earth's surface or underground. There are at least five ways of doing surface mining. Basically, diggers must first remove the soil and rocks above the ore. If the ore is hard, it is broken up with the help of explosives.

A wide variety of mining methods also exists for mining ores that are buried deep underground. In most of them, miners have to cut a vertical shaft with horizontal tunnels into the rock. They use explosives to blast the ore free before removing it. This is a dangerous and expensive method of mining metals.

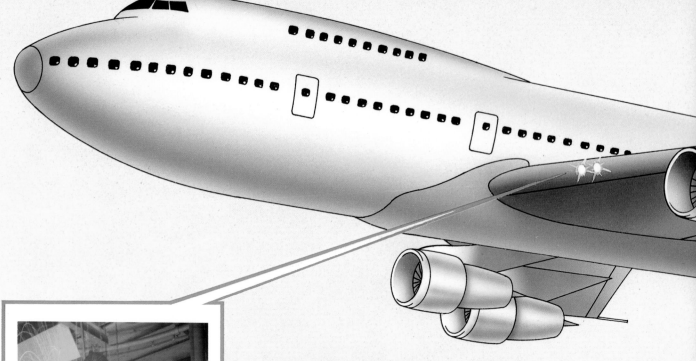

All about metals

Do you know how many different metals are used to build an airplane? There are three main metals. **Aluminum** is needed to make the body of the airplane. A special, strong metal called **titanium** is used to build parts of the airplane's engines. Hundreds of feet of **copper** wire connect all the electrical parts of the airplane.

Where do these different metals come from? They are all found in Earth's crust, either as pieces of pure metal or in minerals that make up ores. Metals can be mixed together to make a new substance called an **alloy**. For example, **bronze** is an alloy of copper and tin.

Metals for different jobs

Some metals are hard and strong but snap easily. These metals are brittle. **Iron** is an example of a brittle metal. Iron is often **alloyed** (combined) with **carbon** and **manganese** to make **steel**. Steel is a hard, strong alloy used to make bridges, railroads, and buildings.

It is easy to work with certain metals, like **gold**, because you can hammer or roll them into shapes, or stretch them and they won't break. Some metals, like **sodium**, are soft, and others, like **mercury**, are liquid.

Copper is found in several different kinds of ore. The rock is removed from the ore and the remaining material passes through a smelter, which removes the copper.

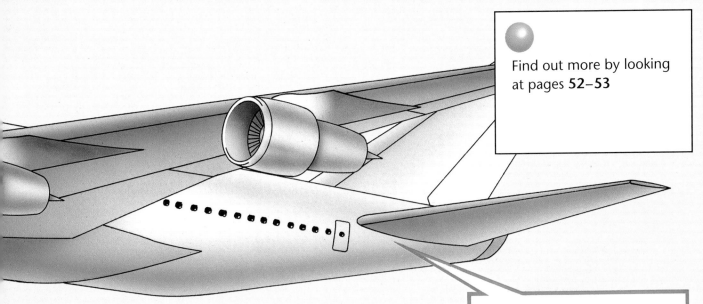

Find out more by looking at pages **52–53**

Tin is an element that comes from the ore **cassiterite**. It is easy to bend but difficult to corrode or wear away. Tin is used to join, or **solder**, metals together. Some cans are made from steel with a thin coating of tin to keep them from rusting. Cans containing soft drinks are made of lightweight aluminum, which comes from an ore called **bauxite**.

Precious metals

We sometimes call valuable metals, such as platinum and gold, **precious metals**. Platinum is the most valuable metal in the world. It is called a **catalyst** because it produces a chemical reaction in other substances without itself changing. Platinum is more expensive than gold and is used in many industries. Another rare metal, **iridium**, is often used as a hardening agent for platinum.

Gold is another valuable metal. It can be rolled and stretched more than any other metal. Gold is used to make jewelry and some electronic equipment. Copper is often added to gold to make it harder.

Another precious metal is silver. Silver must be polished to remove any stains. The photographic film in your camera contains silver, and many ornaments and pieces of jewelry are made of silver.

Aluminum can be flattened between rollers to make sheets of metal. Aluminum sheeting is used on buildings and in machinery, trains, ships, and airplanes.

Gemstones

As molten rock from beneath Earth's surface cools, the minerals inside it may form into **crystals**. These have many different shapes, different numbers of sides, and sharp corners. Some of these crystals are called **gemstones**. They are also known as **gems**.

Gems are very hard. They are sometimes washed into rivers because the surrounding rock where they have formed has worn away. **Diamonds** are the hardest of all known minerals. They formed from carbon millions of years ago. The carbon, surrounded by hot volcanic rock, cooled very slowly and became a diamond.

Many different industries use diamonds because of the hardness of these gems. Diamonds can cut through hard metals quickly and accurately. They are also used in mining and drilling.

Danger: Hot water can scald you! Ask a grown-up to help you with this experiment.

You will need:

hot water

a spoon

a shallow dish

a few drops of food coloring

Epsom salts (magnesium sulfate)

an oven-proof jar

a small bowl

Grow your own crystals

You can grow crystals by evaporating water in which Epsom salts have been dissolved. After a few days in a warm room, the crystals will grow.

1. Put the spoon into the jar and fill the jar with hot water.

2. Add a few spoonfuls of Epsom salts to the water and stir the mixture. Add some more Epsom salts and stir again.

Sapphires come from a mineral called **corundum.** Sapphires exist in all colors of the rainbow. Red sapphires are known as **rubies.** Rubies were used to make the first **lasers.** The ruby crystal helps to produce a strong, thin beam of light that can cut and melt with great accuracy. Lasers are used in industry, in medicine, in communications, and in scientific research.

Diamonds are so hard that one diamond is needed to cut another one. A rough diamond like this can have as many as 58 sides after it has been cut and polished.

4. Place the shallow dish in a place where it will not be disturbed. Pour the mixture into the dish to a depth of about 1/2 inch (1.25 centimeters). Add a few drops of food coloring. Observe how crystals form as the water evaporates. After a few days, you will have a dish of beautiful colored crystals.

3. Fill the bowl with hot water and stand the jar in it. Keep adding more Epsom salts to the jar and keep stirring until the Epsom salts stop dissolving in the water. Allow the liquid to cool.

1. Place a very small sample on an old dish and place it in a cold oven. Heat up the oven, then switch it off and wait until it is cool before removing the sample. **Do this with adult supervision.**

Survey of materials

There are so many different things in the world around us. Some are natural and some are artificial, meaning that people made them. Some were once alive, and others never have been. There are solids and liquids and gases. But everything you look at must have come from either the land, the sea, or the air. These three parts of the world provide us with all the different materials we need.

Before we can use materials, we have to know their qualities, or **properties.** Otherwise, we could make something from the wrong materials and it wouldn't work properly. Imagine this book made from sheets of steel rather than from sheets of paper!

A good way to understand materials and their uses is to look at their properties. This means seeing what a material does when you test it. Simple tests include heating, bending, hammering, scratching, and placing in water.

3. Wrap each sample in a cloth and hit it with a hammer. Does it shatter? **Do this with adult supervision.**

2. Try bending a larger sample with your hands.

4. Leave each sample in a bowl of water. Does it float or sink? Does it change if you leave it there for a few days?

Testing the properties of different materials

Try collecting 20 or more materials from in and around your home. It is best to start with simple materials like a piece of wood, a spoonful of salt, or a pebble. Try not to collect things that are made up of more than one material.

The **data sheet** shown below will help you to organize your collection and to discover the properties of each material. Some materials have already been written down and described on the sheet to show you how. Draw up your own data sheet using these ideas as a starting point. With practice, you can invent your own tests to suit the types of material in your collection. If you do invent your own test, **always check with an adult first**, to make sure it is safe to do.

Make sure you ask an adult to check that your tests are safe and to help you with your activities.

When you have tested your materials, fill in the results on your data sheet. Your list of results will be the different properties of the material.

	Material	Heating not burning	Bending	Hammering	Adding water	Natural, artificial, or both?	Metallic, non-metallic, or both?
1.	Wood	burns	Splinters	dents	floats	natural	non-metallic
2.	Salt	nothing	—	powders	dissolves	natural	metallic
3.	pebbles						
4.	tin lid						
5.	aluminum foil						
6.							
7.							
8.							

60

Find out more by looking
at pages **50–51**
52–53

Resources from our planet

Everything we use each day comes from either the land, the ocean, or the air. Metals are made from ores dug out of the ground. Some medicines contain chemicals found in seawater. Crops are grown with the help of fertilizers that contain nitrogen from the atmosphere and hydrogen from natural gas. Electricity is generated from the energy in coal. Cars and trucks run on fuel made from crude oil. Coal, oil, and natural gas are all **fossil fuels** that are found beneath Earth's surface.

All the materials that we take out of the ground, the ocean, or the air are called **resources.** We are steadily using them up.

Coal is a fossil fuel used mainly to produce electricity. Earth has only a limited supply of fossil fuels.

Renewable resources, like trees, can be replaced. They will never run out if we keep planting new ones.

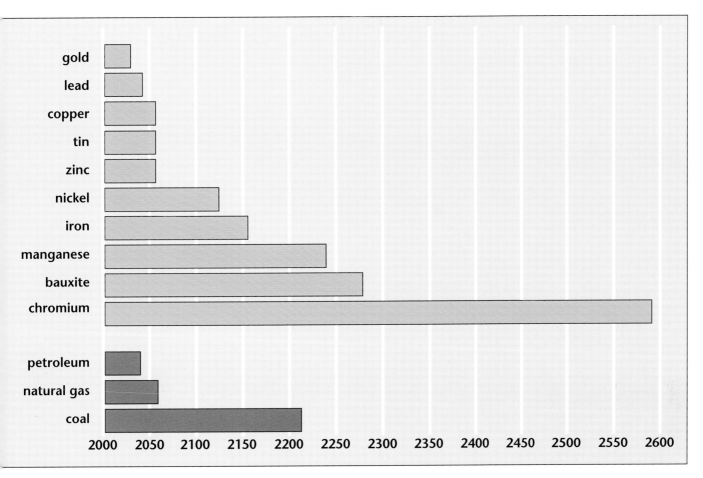

This chart shows how long the world's resources of certain minerals and fossil fuels will last, if we continue to use them as fast as we are doing today.

Nonrenewable and renewable resources

There is a vast amount of air in the atmosphere—about 5 trillion tons! There is even more water in the oceans. We may never use up all the resources in the air and in the oceans. But there is a danger that we may pollute the air and oceans and therefore make them useless.

Resources such as metal ores, coal, oil, and natural gas formed in the ground millions of years ago. As we use them, they are not being replaced, or renewed. We say that these resources are **nonrenewable.**

Other resources are **renewable**, which means they can be replaced. We can generate electricity from the power of the wind or the waves. Hot rocks deep inside Earth's crust can be used to boil water to make steam. This steam can turn a turbine and generate electricity. We can keep growing trees and other plants and use them to make paper and wood products, fuels, and chemicals.

WATER

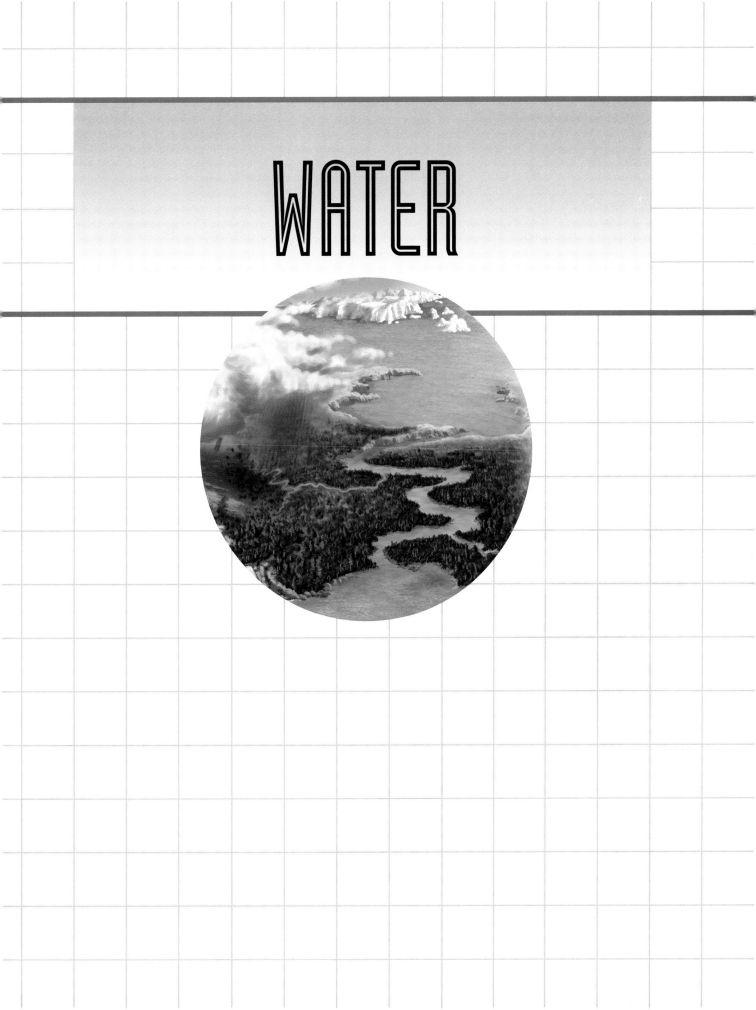

Water everywhere

Did you know that more than 70 percent of Earth's surface is covered with water? There are vast oceans like the Atlantic and the Pacific, and smaller seas like the South China Sea and the Red Sea. There are lakes, rivers, and streams. Around the North and South poles, frozen water forms icecaps that last all year around.

Below ground, there is even more water. This water has soaked down through the soil to fill the spaces between the rocks.

There is even water in the air. Clouds are made up of millions of tiny droplets of water or particles of ice. Clear skies contain moisture which moves around in the air as an invisible gas.

Liquid, solid, or gas?

Water is different from every other substance on Earth because it can be found in its natural state in three different forms. When we speak of water, we usually mean water as a **liquid.** When water is solid, we call it **ice.** When it is a gas, we call it **water vapor.**

Water can change very easily from one form to another. Heat from the sun makes liquid water change to water vapor. When the water vapor cools, it forms rain, which falls to the ground. If it is very cold, the water falls as snow or hail.

All living things need water

Every living thing on Earth depends on water. Animals need water to drink. They may eat other animals or plants, and these also need water to survive and grow. Even plants that live in desert regions, where rain rarely falls, need the tiny amounts of water vapor in the atmosphere to survive.

66

Find out more by looking
at pages **86–87**

The water merry-go-round

When you ride on a merry-go-round, you
pass the same things again and again as it
turns. The way that water travels from the
land to the sky, and then back to the ground,
is something like the circular movement of a
merry-go-round. This circular movement of
water is called the **water cycle**.

When the sun warms the surface waters of the
ocean, some of the water changes into water
vapor. We call this process **evaporation**.
Water vapor rises high in the air. As it rises, it
loses its heat to the surrounding air and
changes back into liquid. At first, these tiny
water droplets hang in the air in clouds. Then
they collect together and form large drops.
We call this process **condensation**. When
conditions in the atmosphere are right, the
drops then fall to the ground as rain. In colder
weather, the water drops may freeze and fall
as hail, sleet, or snow.

Most of the rain falls on the oceans, but much
of it also falls on land and drains into rivers
or streams. Some soaks down through the
soil and rock and gathers underground as
groundwater. In time, this groundwater may
seep out into rivers, but some will stay
underground for years.

*In the water cycle, water moves
through the land and air in different
forms.*

**Water vapor
rises into the air.**

**Plants transpire
moisture into the
atmosphere.**

**The sun heats the
surface of the ocean.**

Plants and the water cycle

Plants play a part in the water cycle, too. They take in water from the ground and release it as moisture through their leaves and other green parts into the atmosphere. This is called **transpiration**. You can watch transpiration at work.

You will need:

a few freshly picked green vegetables or leaves

a medium-sized, dry, plastic food bag

a rubber band

1. Place the vegetables or leaves in the food bag. Seal the top tightly with the rubber band.

2. Put the bag on the window sill for a day. When you look again, you will see that there are drops of water on the inside of the bag. The vegetables or leaves have transpired. Because the leaves and vegetables have been picked, they cannot take in more moisture from the soil. Soon the transpiration will stop.

Water falls as rain, hail, sleet, or snow.

Animals and plants take in water.

Animals lose water.

Find out more by looking at pages **72–73**

Flowing water

Everything on Earth is pulled downward by a special kind of force called **gravity.** It is gravity that tries to pull water toward Earth's center when it falls as rain.

Water always runs downhill. It will settle at the lowest level it can reach, gathering in low-lying places on Earth's surface to form rivers, lakes, and oceans.

Water finds its own level

Have you ever watched a large truck dumping gravel or sand? The gravel pours onto the ground and forms a high mound. It will take a bulldozer or several strong people to rake the gravel flat. But no matter how much water is poured onto the ground, it will never form a pile. Water always settles down to the lowest level possible.

Water thunders over a high cliff in a spectacular waterfall at Antalya, in Turkey.

What happens when you tip water?

Try this experiment. You will need a clear, plastic bottle half filled with water. Make sure you hold the bottle over a sink or bathtub, or else try the experiment outside. Slowly tip the bottle. Does the surface of the water tilt as the bottle tilts? No matter how much you tip the bottle, the surface of the water will always stay level, or horizontal.

Can you make water flow upward?

Although you can't make the surface of water tilt, you can make it flow upward. To do this you will have to make a **siphon**.

You will need:

two short, wide glasses

two thick books

some plastic or rubber tubing

clothespins

1. Fill one of the glasses almost to the top with water and stand it on the books.

2. Put the other glass on the table beside the books.

3. Fill the tubing with water and pinch the ends tightly so the water doesn't run out. (Use clothespins if you find it hard to hold both ends of the tubing closed.)

4. Put one end of the tubing underwater in the full glass, and let go of that end. Make sure the end doesn't flop out of the water.

5. Bend the tubing and put the other end in the empty glass.

6. Let go and watch the water flow from the full glass to the empty glass. Does the water flow only downward to the empty glass?

How does it work?

Gravity pulls the water down to the lowest level of the tubing. At the same time, air pressure is pushing down on the surface of the water in the upper glass. Gravity and air pressure work together to create the flow of water through the siphon.

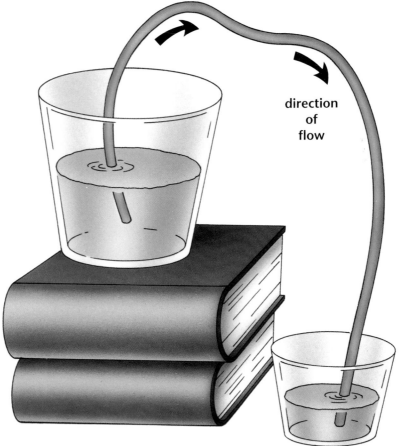

direction of flow

Filling and emptying

Guess the water level

Pour water into different containers and try to guess where the water level will be.

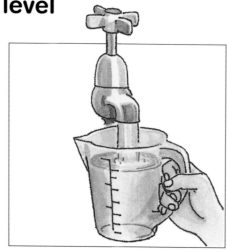

You will need:

a number of jars and bottles of different sizes

a small measuring cup

water

a permanent-ink felt-tipped pen

1. Fill the measuring cup to the top mark with water.

2. Using the felt-tipped pen, mark each of the other containers with a line to show where you think the water level will be. Now pour a full measuring cup of water into each container.

3. How well did you guess the water levels? You will probably find that the water level in some containers is lower than you expected. In other containers, it may be higher.

How did the shape of the container affect your thinking about the level of water each container would reach?

You will need:

Adult supervision

water

a hammer

a small nail

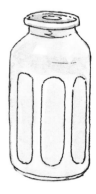

a jar with a tight-fitting lid

Trapped in the bottle

When you pour water from a bottle, you hear a gurgling sound. This sound is made as air enters the bottle to replace the water that you have poured out. If the neck of the bottle is very narrow, air cannot enter the bottle easily. The water coming out and the air going in are fighting for space in the narrow neck. If the hole is very small, the water will not come out at all. You can try this for yourself.

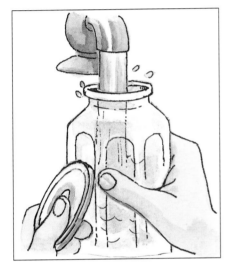

1. Fill the jar with water and screw the lid on firmly.

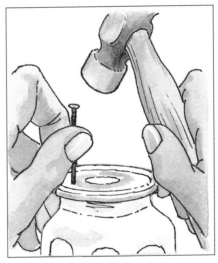

2. With the hammer and nail, make a small hole to one side of the lid. **Ask an adult to help you.**

3. Hold the jar upside down. The water will not drip out. The hole is too small for both the air and water to use.

4. Make a second hole on the other side of the lid and hold the jar upside down again, tilted to one side. This time, water will come out of one hole while air enters through the other.

Underground water

Everything on Earth, including water, is affected by the force of gravity. In trying to pull water down toward Earth's center, gravity pulls water into the ground. As water meets soil and rock, some soils let water soak through them. They are called **porous** soils. **Nonporous** soils do not let water pass through. Do you think bricks are porous or non-porous? How about stones? The activity below will help you find out.

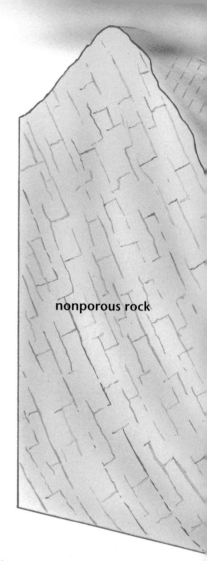

nonporous rock

Underground water collects above nonporous rock in many places on Earth. It is moving, but it may take thousands of years to flow to the sea.

Soaking through

You will need:

two shallow trays

some large stones or pebbles

water

a clay brick

1. Place the brick in one tray and the stones or pebbles in the other.

2. Pour water into each tray until it is about 2 inches (5 centimeters) deep. Leave them for about an hour.

When you go to see what has happened, what do you find? The water around the pebbles looks like it is at the same level. But the water in the brick's tray will be much lower.

The brick is made of baked clay. Baked clay is porous. Regular clay is not so porous. There are tiny holes between the particles of baked clay through which water can move.

If you kept on soaking the brick in water, all the holes would become full of water. The brick would not be able to soak up any more water. But if you placed the wet brick on top of a dry brick on a dry surface, gravity would pull the water down to the second brick.

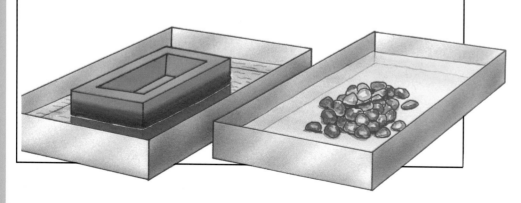

rainfall

Find out more by looking
at pages **66–67**

lake

porous rock

spring

groundwater trapped above
nonporous rock

Porous rock

What happens when rain water soaks into the ground? Most
soil is porous. So are some kinds of rock. Other kinds of rock
are nonporous. Gravity makes rain water soak into most
soils and also into porous rock. Once the soil and rock have
become full of water, they cannot soak up any more water.
They let the water pass through until it reaches nonporous
rock. Then it can go no farther. The water gathers in the
spaces between the rocks as groundwater.

There are great stores of groundwater all over the world. This
groundwater sometimes escapes through holes in the surface
to make a spring. Or else we can dig a well to reach it.

Safe to drink?

Women collect water for drinking and cooking from the river at the Garisar Gate in Jaisalmer, India.

If you have ever been swimming in the ocean, you will know that seawater tastes salty. Almost all the water that covers our planet—about 97 percent of it—is seawater.

Seawater is not good to drink. Few plants can live in it, and it cannot be used in most factories or homes. Fortunately, the remaining 3 percent of the world's water is fresh water. This means that it is not salty, and if it is clean, it can be used for drinking, cooking, and washing.

Find out more by looking at pages **72–73**
82–83

Do not drink the filtered water. Germs and harmful chemicals can still pass through the filter and stay in the water.

Storing water

In many parts of the world, people collect and store river water and rain water. In other places, groundwater which lies trapped in rocks underground is pumped to the surface. People living in towns and cities use enormous amounts of water. It is sometimes drawn from nearby rivers and stored in huge, artificial lakes called **reservoirs.**

Most water is not safe to drink straight from the reservoir. It contains harmful substances. This water is pumped from the reservoir to a **water treatment plant,** where particles of soil and plant material are removed, or **filtered** out. At the same time, a small amount of a gas called **chlorine** is pumped in to kill any harmful bacteria. After this, the water can be pumped through underground pipes to our faucets.

Making water clean

One way of taking soil and plant material out of water is to filter it. Make your own filter using sand, gravel, pebbles, and cotton.

You will need:

scissors

absorbent cotton

a glass

small pebbles

gravel

sand

water

a small pitcher

a teaspoon

soil

a plastic bottle
or a funnel

1. Cut off the bottom of the plastic bottle with your scissors. Ask an adult to help you.

2. Push some absorbent cotton into the neck. Turn the bottle upside down and put it into the glass. (The fit between the bottle and the glass should be tight but not too tight. If the fit is not good, use a funnel instead of the bottle.)

3. Fill the bottle with layers of small pebbles, then gravel, then sand. All these materials must be clean.

4. Pour some water into the pitcher. Put in two teaspoons of soil and stir it well.

5. Pour some of the soil and water mixture onto the sand in the bottle.

6. Watch the water drip into the glass.

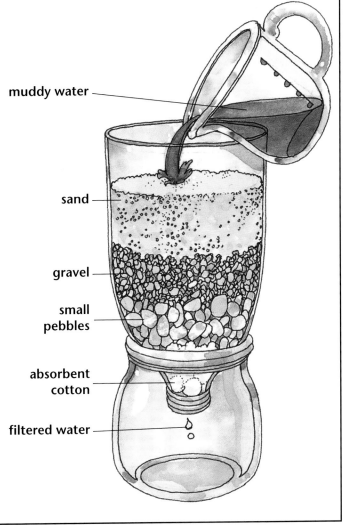

muddy water

sand

gravel

small pebbles

absorbent cotton

filtered water

Using water

In some parts of the world, water is so scarce that people often use it more than once before throwing it away. For example, they might save water used in cooking and wash the dishes with it.

Water at home

In countries where the water supply is piped straight to homes, people are less concerned about how much water they use. The most water is used in the world's major cities. Each person in the United States uses an average of more than 100 gallons (380 liters) of water every day. People in London, in the United Kingdom, each use about 40 gallons (150 liters) of water a day. In these places, people are so used to having plenty of water that they are very surprised if there is a shortage of water after a period of dry weather.

In most cities, water is stored outside the cities and piped directly into homes. People expect that there will be water every time they turn on the faucet.

Factories use water

A lot more water is used in factories than in our homes. Almost all the food made in factories, from bread to hamburgers, contains water. Apart from this, water is used in most factory work to wash materials, cool down machines, and clean factory equipment. Factories in the United States use about 160 billion gallons (600 billion liters) of water every day.

At the printing plant, 80 gallons (300 liters) of water are used to make the paper for one Sunday newspaper.

Water is essential for manufacturing. Most of the water in factories is used for cooling equipment.

In Sudan, there may be less than 1.3 gallons (5 liters) of water a day for each person.

How much water do you use each day?

40 gallons (152 liters)

15 gallons (57 liters)

7 gallons (36 liters)

20–30 gallons (76–114 liters)

Irrigation

Water is needed to grow healthy crops. Sometimes, it has to be brought to land that would otherwise be too dry. Taking water to the land is called **irrigation.**

About 550 million acres (220 million hectares) of the world's farmland is irrigated. This is an area about two-thirds the size of Africa. A great deal of this irrigated land is used for growing rice, which is the main food of nearly half the people in the world.

These rice fields in the mountains of Bali, in Indonesia, have been irrigated with rain water.

Water for people

Without enough water, the human body is soon unable to go on working. Our blood is mostly made of water. Blood carries oxygen from our lungs and **nutrients** from our intestines to all parts of our bodies. Nutrients are the useful chemicals that we take from our food. Water also helps to keep our muscles and joints running smoothly.

Some of this water is lost because we breathe it out. In cold weather, we can see the water vapor condensing in the cold air as it comes out of our mouths. We lose water when we perspire and when we go to the toilet. If we are ill, we often have a fever and perspire more than usual. This is why, if you are ill, the doctor may tell you to drink plenty of liquids.

Watery you!

Did you know that you could live without water for only about a week? You probably think your body feels firm and solid because it's full of strong bone and muscle. But, in fact, about 65 percent of your body is made up of water. Because we lose water, we need to keep replenishing the water in our bodies. We need about 2.5 quarts (2.4 liters) of water each day.

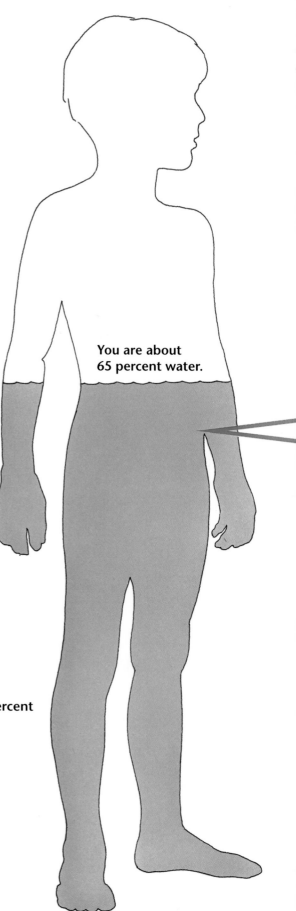

You are about 65 percent water.

An elephant is made up of about 70 percent water.

A jellyfish is about 95 percent water.

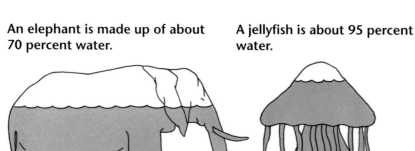

Find out more by looking at pages **80–81**

water
100%

milk
95%

Drink up!

We may drink water from the tap or from a bottle. We may drink it in lemonade or fruit juice. Some of our solid food contains a great deal of water. Water makes up about 85 percent of an apple or an orange, and about 95 percent of a head of lettuce.

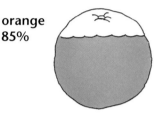

orange
85%

How much water do you drink?

Keep a record of how much water you drink in one day.

potato
80%

You will need:

a measuring cup

a notebook

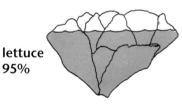

lettuce
95%

1. Use a kitchen measuring cup to measure every drink you have. Remember to measure dairy drinks, because milk is about 95 percent water.

bread
30%

2. Make a note of each measurement and write it in your notebook.

You will probably be surprised when you add up the total at the end of the day. But this will tell you only part of the story. You have also taken in lots of water in the solid food you have eaten.

tomato
95%

steak
73%

Lots to drink

Did you know that every person in the world takes in about 16,000 gallons (60,600 liters) of water during his or her lifetime?

80

Find out more by looking
at pages **72–73**
92–93
108–109

*Spring water comes from deep
underground. It is full of minerals
dissolved from the rocks and can be
very good to drink. Sometimes it is
bottled straight from the spring.*

Water is good for you

The water you drink from the faucet has come
a long way. It has traveled as rain through the
atmosphere. It has flowed along the ground
into a river. It may have spent part of its
journey underground.

On the way, it has picked up many
substances, which have **dissolved** in the
water. This means that the substances are
broken down into tiny particles. The particles
and the water form a **solution**.

Some substances that dissolve in water are
minerals. Minerals are chemicals that come
from rocks. Some may be harmful, and water
containing them is not used for drinking.
Other minerals are essential for good health.

Minerals for health

We need to take in large amounts of some
minerals each day. One of these is **calcium.**
It is found in foods like cheese, but also in
milk and water. We need only a small
amount of other minerals to keep us healthy.
These are often called **trace elements,**
because we need only a trace, meaning a
small amount. **Fluorine,** in the form of the
chemical compound fluoride, is one trace
element that may be found in water. Fluoride
helps us grow strong teeth.

Many doctors believe that the water in some
places is more healthful than the water in
others. This is because there is a higher
percentage of beneficial minerals and trace
elements dissolved in the water.

We also get minerals from plants. Plants take
minerals out of the water in the soil. When
we eat the plants, the minerals are
passed on to us.

Water from the spring at Buxton in the United Kingdom is bottled at this bottling factory. The spring water does not need to be filtered and treated. It is bottled directly from the spring.

Down the drain

It's amazing to think about how many ways we use water every day. Not only do we drink water to stay healthy, we use it for bathing, flushing the toilet, washing clothes, cooking, and dishwashing.

Used water most often goes down the drain. It contains soaps and detergents, human waste, pieces of leftover food, and many other solids and liquids. This waste water is called **sewage**. It usually contains harmful bacteria that could spread disease, so it has to be **treated** (cleaned) carefully. If sewage and waste water are dumped without having been treated, they cause **pollution**. There are too many harmful substances and bacteria in sewage. Waste water disturbs the balance of life in rivers and lakes.

In some countries, untreated sewage is allowed to flow straight into rivers or into the ocean, where it causes pollution. A better way of dealing with waste water is to pipe it to a sewage treatment plant.

settling tank

1. At a sewage treatment plant, the sewage flows into a settling tank. The solids in the water sink to the bottom and form a thick sludge.

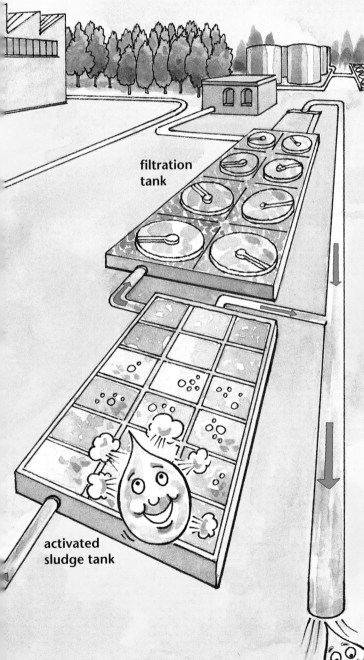

filtration tank

activated sludge tank

2. In some sewage treatment plants, the water is trickled slowly through filtration tanks where bacteria feed on the decaying material.

3. In modern sewage treatment plants, the liquid goes to an activated sludge tank where air is bubbled through it. This helps the bacteria in the tank feed quickly on the harmful substances.

4. The water is now clean enough to be pumped into lakes, oceans, rivers, and streams. It will rejoin the water cycle. Eventually, it may be used again—you might even drink it!

Changing water

Water is one of the most common and unusual substances on Earth. No other substance can change its shape and form like water can.

Water, like all substances, is made up of tiny particles called **molecules.** A single drop of water contains millions of molecules. Each of these molecules is made up of even smaller particles. These are called **atoms.** Each water molecule contains atoms of two substances, **hydrogen** and **oxygen.** Two atoms of hydrogen join with one atom of oxygen to form water. Scientists give hydrogen the symbol **H** and oxygen **O.** These symbols are used together to give the scientific name for water—H_2O. Can you see why?

The three states of water

Water can exist in three states—a solid, a liquid, or a gas. The molecules that make up liquid water are always moving freely. When water is cold, the molecules slow down. If cooled enough, water can change to ice. When rain water is frozen, it takes on other forms, such as snow, hail, or sleet.

When water is heated to a boiling state, it forms steam. The molecules move around in the air with great speed and a high level of energy.

Water will always flow to the lowest place it can reach. At the Iguaçu Falls, on the border of Brazil and Argentina, the water falls more than 231 feet (70 meters).

When water freezes, the molecules slow down and form a regular pattern. Snowflakes such as these always have six sides, though each one is different from any other.

Millions of droplets of boiling water and steam from the Old Faithful geyser, in Yellowstone National Park, come from inside Earth's crust.

The tiny droplets of water in this dawn fog in the Namib Desert, in southwestern Africa, will gradually evaporate as the day becomes hotter.

These icicles are solid water and very hard. As water trickles down from the eave, it freezes into an icicle. Then, as more water trickles down, it freezes and adds to the size of the icicles.

This snowman contains millions of tiny ice crystals, but most of it is air.

Drying up

Water is constantly on the move, in the oceans and rivers, in a pond that looks completely still, even in a glass of water. Water molecules are always moving around at different speeds. If they move fast enough, some break away from the surface and enter the air. This is called **evaporation.** Some of the molecules then fall back into the water. But others become water vapor and are carried away by air currents. In this way some of the water is gradually lost to the atmosphere.

You can see this happen if you leave a saucer of water uncovered indoors. After a time, there will be no water left in the saucer. It will all have evaporated.

Wet laundry on a clothesline dries more quickly in a breeze. The wind carries away the water molecules soon after they enter the air from the washing. Hardly any of them fall back on the clothes.

Evaporation and condensation

When water is heated, all of its molecules speed up and more of them escape. If water is made hot enough, all the molecules eventually escape and the water boils away. All of it becomes water vapor.

Heat speeds up evaporation. Cold slows it down and may even reverse it, turning the water vapor back into water droplets. This process is called **condensation.** When you take a hot bath, molecules from the bathwater escape into the air and become water vapor. Some of them touch the cold bathroom walls and windows, and this cools them down and turns them back into drops of water. The walls, windows, and bathroom mirror become misty.

The insides of windows sometimes become misty on rainy days for the same reason. Inside a warm room, molecules of water vapor are moving around. Some of them meet the glass of the windows, which the rain has cooled. The loss of heat turns the water vapor near the glass back into water. If it gets cold enough at night, the water on the window will freeze and you may wake up to find your windows are frosty on the inside!

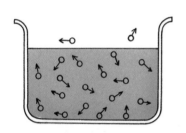

When water is cold, very few molecules will evaporate.

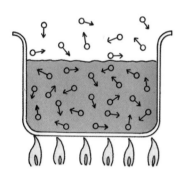

When water is warmed, the water molecules will escape more quickly from the surface into the air.

Find out more by looking at pages **66–67**

These wet clothes will dry faster when the wind is blowing. The water molecules evaporate into the air and are blown away by the wind.

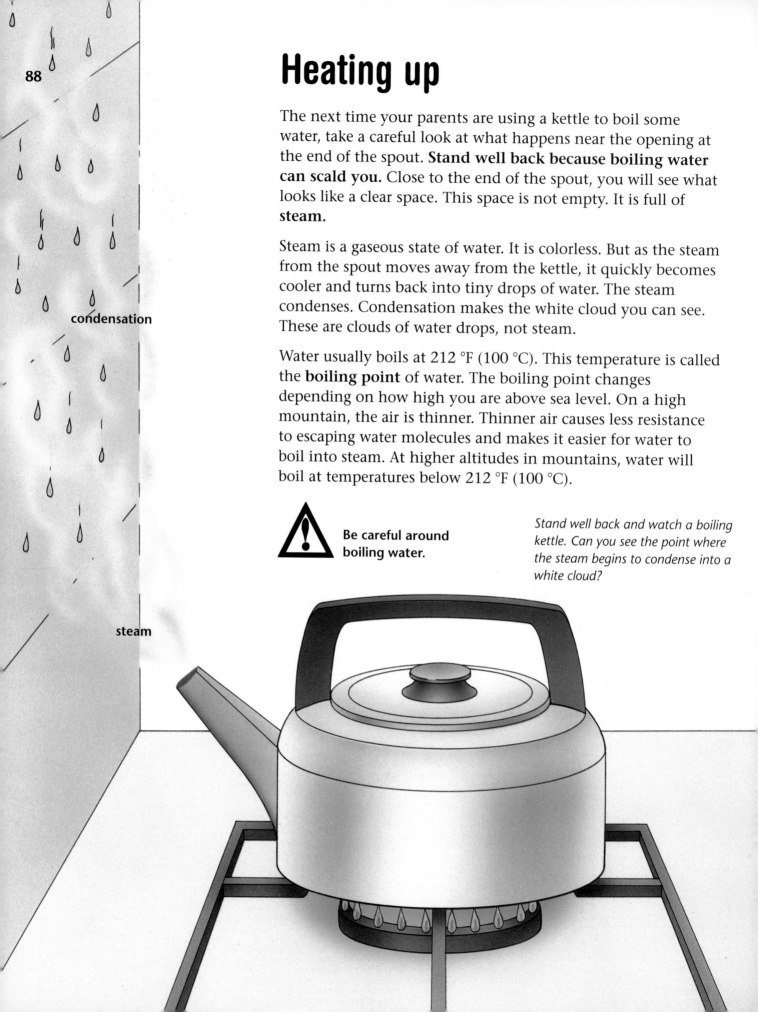

condensation

steam

Heating up

The next time your parents are using a kettle to boil some water, take a careful look at what happens near the opening at the end of the spout. **Stand well back because boiling water can scald you.** Close to the end of the spout, you will see what looks like a clear space. This space is not empty. It is full of **steam**.

Steam is a gaseous state of water. It is colorless. But as the steam from the spout moves away from the kettle, it quickly becomes cooler and turns back into tiny drops of water. The steam condenses. Condensation makes the white cloud you can see. These are clouds of water drops, not steam.

Water usually boils at 212 °F (100 °C). This temperature is called the **boiling point** of water. The boiling point changes depending on how high you are above sea level. On a high mountain, the air is thinner. Thinner air causes less resistance to escaping water molecules and makes it easier for water to boil into steam. At higher altitudes in mountains, water will boil at temperatures below 212 °F (100 °C).

Be careful around boiling water.

Stand well back and watch a boiling kettle. Can you see the point where the steam begins to condense into a white cloud?

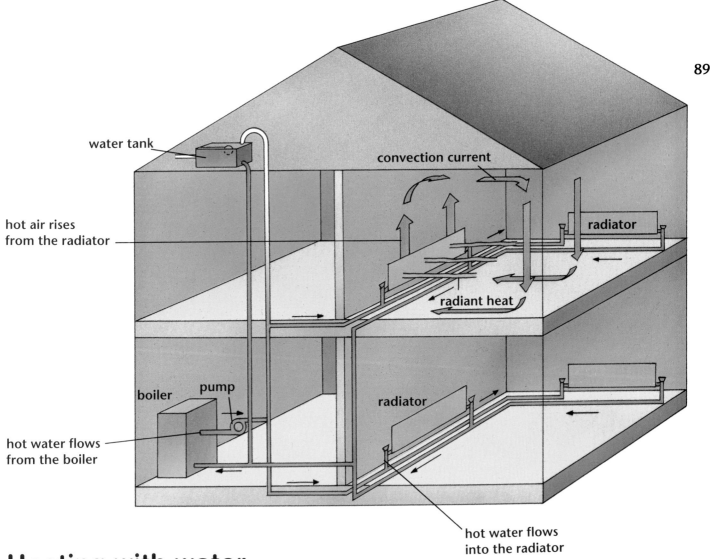

water tank

convection current

radiator

hot air rises
from the radiator

radiant heat

boiler

pump

radiator

hot water flows
from the boiler

hot water flows
into the radiator

Heating with water

Hot water or steam in pipes is a convenient way of moving heat around buildings. This is what some central heating systems do. The water is heated up in a boiler and pumped through pipes to radiators in each room. Heat travels from the water into the metal of the radiators. Moving heat from one object to another in this way is called **conduction.**

Now the heat travels from the radiators to warm the air in the room. It does this in two ways. One is by a movement called **convection.** The radiator heats the air around it. The heated air rises, and cool air rushes in to take its place. The hot air moves along the ceiling away from the radiator pushing cooler air in front of it. This **convection current** moves down the wall opposite the radiator, along the floor, and back to the radiator again.

A radiator also works by sending out waves of heat in the same way as the sun. This is called **radiant heat.**

Hot air from the radiator moves around the room. The heat is gradually lost to the cool air by conduction.

Solid water

The **freezing temperature** of water is 32 °F (0 °C). Below this temperature, water vapor on the ground turns to frost and water vapor in the air turns to snowflakes. Liquid water changes to a solid, such as ice and hail. If the liquid water is flowing, it will need to be much colder before it freezes. The still water of a lake will turn to ice more quickly than the moving water of a river.

The continent of Antarctica, at the South Pole, is covered by an ice sheet with an average thickness of 7,100 feet (2,200 meters). Around the coast the ice is thinner, and bits often break off to make icebergs, which float away.

Swollen water

Water is an unusual substance because the liquid increases in **volume** when it changes to ice. When water freezes, the water molecules lock together in a certain pattern, which takes up more room than liquid water. You can see this when a full bottle of water freezes. The ice takes up more room. It may come out of the top, or it may break the bottle.

If you float an ice cube in water, more than three-quarters of it is below the water level. Icebergs are dangerous to ships because most of an iceberg is hidden below the waterline.

How do you make ice melt?

One way to make ice melt is to put it somewhere warm. Another way is to squeeze it, or to put **pressure** on it. Have you ever skated on ice? When you skate, all your weight pushes down on the thin blades of the skates. Your weight puts a large amount of pressure on a small, thin area of the ice. This pressure makes the ice melt. As you glide along, the surface instantly melts beneath the blades. You are really skating on a very thin line of water. This water freezes again as you move on, and the pressure is released.

91

Find out more by looking at pages **84–85**

Finding out about ice

Here are some experiments you can do with ice.

You will need:

an ice cube

a small, strong, plastic bottle

a glove

a spoon and a saucer

2. Now put the saucer in the freezer overnight. Take the saucer out the next morning. Using the glove to protect your hand, put the ice cube on the cold saucer.

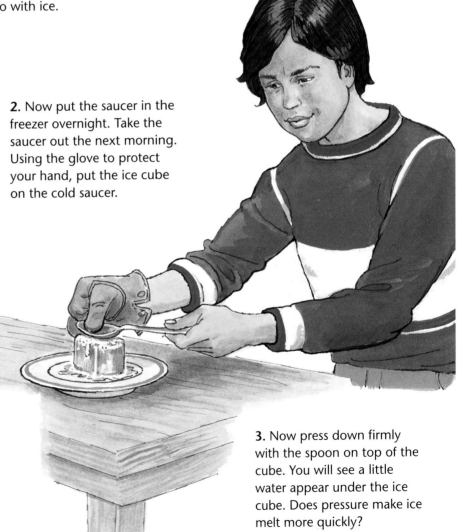

1. Fill the plastic bottle to the top with water. Place it in the freezer overnight. In the morning, the water will be frozen, and the ice will stick out from the top of the bottle. Does water increase in volume when it freezes?

3. Now press down firmly with the spoon on top of the cube. You will see a little water appear under the ice cube. Does pressure make ice melt more quickly?

Find out more by looking at pages **94–95**

Water for growth

When you look at some flower seeds, it's often hard to imagine that they can grow into the lovely flowers in the picture on the packet. Seeds look as if they have no life in them at all.

However, seeds have all the food they need to start growing. So why don't they grow inside their packet? Seeds need three other things to begin growing. They need oxygen, warmth, and water. If they have these three things, the seeds start growing. They use the nutrients stored inside them, the water they absorb from the soil, and the oxygen they take from the air. Some seeds stay dormant for up to 50 years before they start growing, and then only if the conditions for growth are right.

There is only a small amount of nutrients inside each seed. When these nutrients are all used up, plants must make their own food.

Seeds must wait for the right conditions before they start growing.

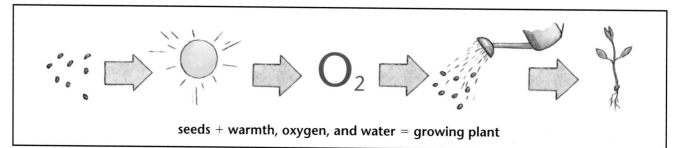

seeds + warmth, oxygen, and water = growing plant

Food from the soil

Plants get their food from the soil. They soak up water from the soil through their roots. This water has nutrients dissolved in it. Not all soil contains the nutrients that plants need. Sometimes a farmer or gardener has to add these nutrients to the soil in the form of **mineral** or **organic fertilizers.** Mineral fertilizers come from minerals or chemicals. Organic fertilizers come from decayed plant or animal matter. The fertilizers are washed into the soil by rain and picked up by the plants' roots.

Farmers spread fertilizer on their land to put more nutrients into the soil. Then they can grow healthier crops.

Growing in the desert

Most plants store water in their roots, stems, and leaves. Each time it rains, they refill their store. But in the desert, it might not rain for many months, or even years. Then it falls as a short, heavy shower. When it rains, the shallow, wide-spreading roots of a cactus can soak up the water very quickly, before it evaporates. The leaves of the cactus become swollen with the extra water. They will act as a water store, supplying the plant with the water it needs. Other desert shrubs send down deep roots to reach groundwater far below the surface.

There are even plants, like the welwitschia of the Namib Desert, that trap the tiny droplets of water which form when the desert fog condenses. The water collects in their twisted leaves and trickles down to the roots.

Desert plants have special roots to cope with infrequent rainfall or to reach water lying deep underground.

Watch roots grow

Fill a jar almost full of water. Place an onion in the neck of the jar. Make sure its base is in the water.

Watch the onion roots grow.

A cactus has shallow roots.

This shrub has wide-spreading roots.

This shrub has deep roots.

The welwitschia catches water in its leaves.

Find out more by looking
at pages **92–93**

Drawn upward

When we feel thirsty, we have a drink. We take water into our bodies by swallowing it. Plants don't swallow. So how do they take in water? On a plant's roots, there are tiny growths called **root hairs.** Plants take in water and nutrients through their root hairs, using a process called **osmosis.**

Osmosis is the movement of liquid from one **solution** into another through a **membrane** that separates them. A solution is a mixture of a liquid and some dissolved substances. A membrane is a thin "skin" that allows some substances, but not others, to pass through.

During osmosis, water containing nutrients moves from the soil, through membranes covering the root hairs, and into the roots. The membranes allow the water to seep into the root hairs, and also prevent nutrient-rich liquid from leaving the roots.

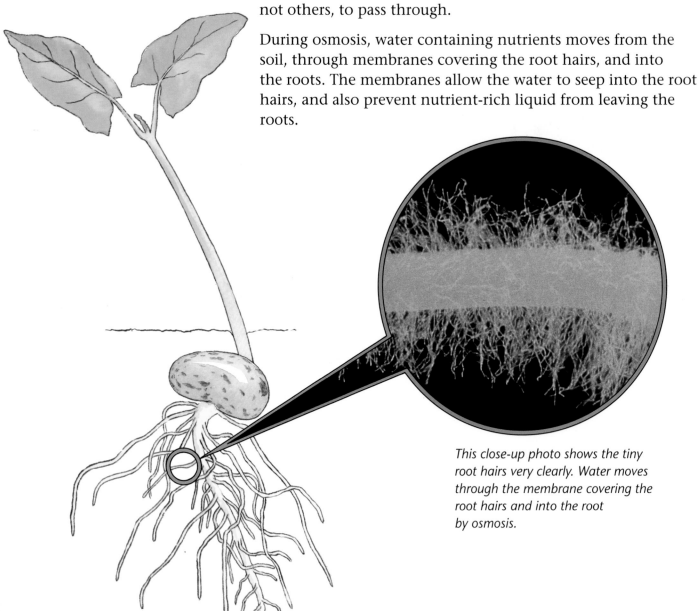

This close-up photo shows the tiny root hairs very clearly. Water moves through the membrane covering the root hairs and into the root by osmosis.

Sap

Water enters the plant through its root hairs. As the water moves from the root hairs, into the roots, and up into the stem or trunk of a plant, it thickens into a nutrient-rich liquid that "feeds" the plant. We call this liquid **sap**.

If you cut off the stem of some plants, such as the sugar cane, you will see a drop of sap forming at the cut end. This sap contains sugars that feed the plant, and we can use it to make sugar. Some plants contain other liquids that we can use. We can make rubber out of the milky liquid that oozes out of rubber trees.

Liquid rubber is tapped from a rubber tree in Malaysia. The liquid comes from beneath the bark and is collected in a cup.

Looking at osmosis

When does osmosis work? You can find out in this experiment, using any root vegetable, such as a potato or a yam.

You will need:

a knife

one large root vegetable

a spoon

some sugar

a cup

a large dish with a lid

water

1. Ask an adult to cut the vegetable into two large slices or halves for you. Then, hollow out each vegetable slice so that each is about 1 inch (2.5 cm) thick.

2. Dissolve one spoonful of sugar in four spoonfuls of cold water in the cup. This makes a sugary liquid. Half fill one slice with this liquid. Half fill the other slice with cold water.

3. Place both slices in a dish. Pour cold water into the dish to a depth of 1/2 inch (1 centimeter). Cover the dish.

4. Look at the slices after a day. Do you see any difference in their water levels? The level of the sugary liquid will have risen. The water has entered the concentrated sugary liquid by osmosis.

Find out more by looking at pages **86–87**

Water with skin

What do you think happens if you place a needle very carefully on the surface of the water? You'd probably expect it to sink. But it doesn't—it floats. Why does this happen?

The needle is resting on an invisible "skin" that covers the water. This "skin" is made from water molecules clinging together on the surface. Scientists call this **surface tension**. You would have to press the needle down into the water before it would sink.

All the molecules in water cling to each other. If you look at a dripping faucet, you will see that falling drops of water have a roundish shape. While they fall, they are not splattering in all directions. Clinging molecules in the water's surface, as well as high surface tension, are pulling the water into round droplets.

A water strider can walk on the water because of surface tension.

Testing surface tension

You will need:

a needle

a small piece of facial tissue or toilet paper

a glass of water

1. Rub the needle between your fingers to make its surface a little oily.

2. Place the tissue carefully onto the surface of the water.

3. Gently drop the needle onto the tissue while it's still floating. The paper will soak up the water and sink. The needle will be left on the surface, held up by surface tension.

Water that clings

Not only do water molecules cling to each other, they cling even more to the molecules of solid objects. If you pour some colored water into a glass, you can see that some of the water clings to the edge of the glass, so that the surface curves slightly upward near the edges. You can see this even more clearly if you dip a clear plastic drinking straw into water. Pinch the top of the straw and lift it out to eye level. Inside the straw, the surface of the water will be curved.

Water that climbs

Cut a strip of tissue paper or blotting paper, and dip the end in water. You will see the water climb up through the paper. The paper has tiny holes in it, and the water molecules move up to fill the holes. This movement of water molecules is called **capillary action**.

Look carefully at the surface shape of the water in the glass and in the straw. Describe what you see.

Making waves

You will remember that although water seeks the lowest level, this does not mean it is always flat and still. Water is very easily disturbed. Next time you have a glass of water, blow gently across the surface and see what happens. Try sitting in the bath and keeping the water still. You wouldn't be able to move at all. The slightest movement will disturb the water. When you stand up to get out of the bathwater, it is like a storm at sea. The high waves at sea are mostly caused by the wind and by the pull of gravity from the moon and the sun.

Ripples

If you throw a stone into a puddle, ripples spread out from where it hits the water. These ripples are like circular ridges of water that spread out in larger and larger circles to the edge of the puddle.

Although it looks as if the water is moving outward, it's not. It is only this wave shape on the surface that moves.

The bobbing cork

You can see what is really happening by floating a cork in the water, and then dropping in a stone. When the waves reach the cork, they do not push it along. The cork simply moves up and down as each wave passes underneath it.

Gently use an egg beater to disturb a bowl of water. Can you see any patterns in the way the water moves?

When you throw a stone into water, small waves ripple out in circles.

The cork moves up and down on the water, but it does not move any closer to the edge.

Find out more by looking
at pages **68–69**
            100–101

Ships at sea in rough weather often encounter huge waves. These ships have to be strong enough to take a battering from the waves. They are designed so that they can still function despite the waves.

Powerful waves

Storm waves can be very powerful. Ocean waves can reach heights of 40 feet (12 meters). Such waves have been known to sink ships. Near the shore, waves can pick up huge boulders and hurl them onto the land. Waves can also smash ships against rocks and destroy them.

Waves out at sea behave like the ripples. As waves move forward, the water does not. It moves around and around in a circular, rolling motion.

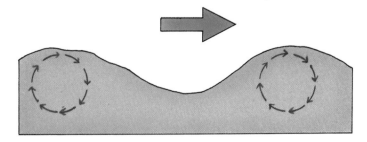

100

Find out more by looking at pages **98–99**

Pushing through water

What kind of shape can push its way through water most efficiently? When something such as a surfboard or a canoe moves through water, the water is pushed aside. It flows around the object, then comes together again behind it. If the water flows smoothly around the object, we say that the shape of the object is **streamlined.** If the shape is not streamlined, the waterflow is disturbed. This disturbance is called **turbulence.** A streamlined shape is rounded at the front, and pointed behind.

Engineers can show how water flows around different shapes by adding streaks of dye to the water. The dye in the water flows evenly until it meets the object and flows around it. The streaks of dye show the shape of the currents that flow around the object. In this way, engineers can tell whether there is a turbulent or streamlined flow of water.

You can see the difference between these two shapes. One can glide easily through the water. The other causes turbulence.

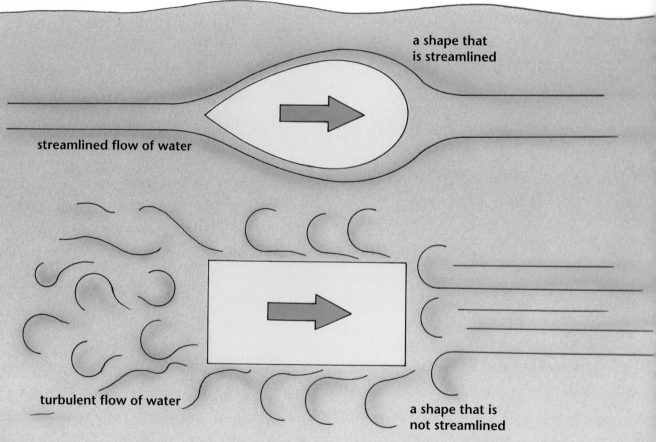

a shape that is streamlined

streamlined flow of water

turbulent flow of water

a shape that is not streamlined

Ships and submarines

Understanding streamlined shapes is important to people who design ships and submarines. When a ship or submarine moves forward, water is pushed aside. If the ship or submarine is well designed, the flow of water around it is streamlined, and it uses energy efficiently. A badly designed ship or submarine causes turbulence. It will use up more energy as it moves through the water.

The streamlined design of this submarine helps it slip through the water easily.

Streamlined fish

There are many reasons why fish have a very streamlined shape. As they move through the water smoothly, they use a minimum of energy. A streamlined shape hardly disturbs the water, so the fishes' prey do not realize their attackers are nearby until it is too late.

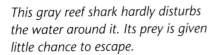

This gray reef shark hardly disturbs the water around it. Its prey is given little chance to escape.

Find out more by looking
at pages **70–71**
        104–105

Sinkers and floaters

Have you learned to swim? Even if learning to swim was easy, it was probably difficult for you to learn how to float. At first, everyone expects to sink to the bottom of the water. It is difficult to believe that the water will hold you up.

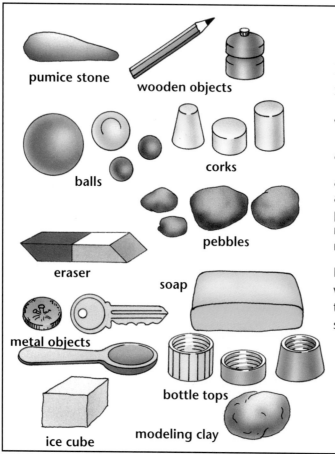

pumice stone

wooden objects

balls

corks

pebbles

eraser

soap

metal objects

bottle tops

ice cube

modeling clay

Sink or float?

Find out if objects will float in water. You may find some surprises!

You will need:

a bowl of water

a collection of objects, such as an ice cube, pebbles, an eraser, pieces of wood, balls of different materials and sizes, and some metal objects, such as keys or coins

Place the objects in the bowl of water one at a time. Make a list of the ones that float and the ones that sink.

Density

Do you know why some things float while others sink? It isn't just because of their size or their weight. If you can float when you go swimming, why does a small pebble sink? The answer is that floating or sinking depends on an object's **density.** If an object is more dense than water, it sinks. If it is less dense than water, it floats.

An object is more dense than water if it weighs more than the same amount, or **volume**, of water. Pebbles are made of gritty particles, which are very heavy and packed together tightly. This is why they sink. They are more dense than water.

Why do ships float?

Steel has a higher density than water, so why doesn't a steel ship sink? The answer is that the inside of a ship is hollow and contains air. It also contains other materials that are less dense than water. The density of the whole ship is less than that of water. You can try this out with an experiment.

Testing density

Test the density of your boat in this experiment.

You will need:

a large lump of modeling clay

a bowl of water

1. Roll the modeling clay into a ball and put it in the water. What happens?

2. Take the clay out, and mold it in the shape of a boat. Put it on the water. What happens? You have the same amount of clay. Explain the difference.

Water takes weight

Find out how water can take some of the weight of heavy objects.

You will need:

a brick or a large stone

string

a rubber band

a bowl of water

Tie a piece of string around the brick. Tie the other end of the string to a rubber band.

Hold the brick by the rubber band and lower it into the water. Is there any difference in the length of the rubber band before and after you put the brick in the water?

After you put the brick in the water, the rubber band will be stretched less. This is because the water is supporting some of the brick's weight.

Most of your body weight is more dense than water. Because your lungs are full of air, your body all together is less dense than water and, therefore, you can float!

A pinch of salt

Put two or three pinches of table salt into half a glass of water and stir the water with a spoon. What happens? The salt seems to disappear. In fact, it is still there, but it has dissolved in the water. The salt and water have formed a solution. Each grain of salt is a crystal. This is a group of particles arranged in a regular pattern. Water molecules break the crystals up into individual salt particles, which are too small to be seen. This is why the salt seems to disappear.

Why is the sea salty?

Most of Earth's surface is covered with a solution. We call this solution seawater. There are many things dissolved in it, but the most common substance is a chemical called **sodium chloride.** We know it better as table salt. It makes the sea taste salty.

You may think the salt has disappeared. But taste the water and you will find the salt is still there. You cannot see it because it has dissolved.

Salt from the ocean

Some of our salt comes from the ocean. First, seawater is allowed to flow into large shallow pools. The heat of the sun evaporates the water, leaving the salt behind.

Too much salt

Substances that dissolve in water are described as **soluble** substances. We can make soluble substances dissolve faster by stirring, shaking, or warming them. What would happen if you continued to put more salt into the water? After a time, no more would dissolve, no matter how much you stirred it, shook it, or warmed it. The solution would be **saturated.** A saturated solution cannot hold any more of a soluble substance.

Salt is collected in these salt pans in Brazil.

Will it dissolve?

Some things will not dissolve in water. They are **insoluble.**

You will need:

a glass

a glass bowl

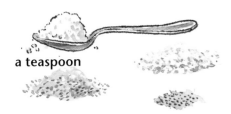

a teaspoon

a collection of different powdered substances, such as sugar, sand, toast crumbs, or pepper

1. Test each substance, one at a time, in a clean glass of water. Stir the water to see if you can make a solution in water. If none of the powder has sunk to the bottom after a few minutes, then it is a soluble powder. Make sure you change the water for each test.

2. Now try mixing some insoluble substances together. Stir them well in a clear bowl of water. Then leave the mixture to settle for an hour. The heaviest particles sink to the bottom. The lighter ones will take longer to sink. You will be able to see different layers.

Dense water

We have seen how some objects float in water and some do not. An object will float if it is less dense than water. But you can make some objects float that would normally sink. How can you do this? We can look at some eggs to find out.

Fresh eggs and rotten eggs

How can you tell a fresh egg from a rotten one? It's easy. Put them in a bowl of water. The fresh egg will sink. But the rotten one will float.

Fresh eggs sink because they are more dense than water. When an egg goes rotten, gas is made and trapped inside. The gas has a lower density than water. This allows the rotten egg to float.

But you can make a fresh egg float by dissolving plenty of salt in the water. The salt makes the water more dense than the egg. Now the egg will float, or become **buoyant.** What if the water is only slightly salty? The egg might float or sink, depending on how salty the water is.

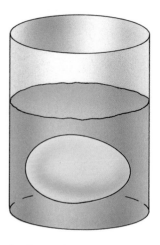

The fresh egg is more dense than the water, so it sinks.

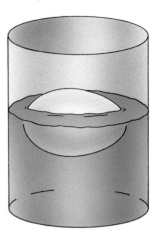

The rotten egg has lots of gas. It is less dense than the fresh egg, so it floats.

Better buoyancy

Try this experiment with a boat made of modeling clay. You will see how fresh water and salt water differ by observing how much weight a clay boat can hold before it sinks.

You will need:

a small bowl of fresh water

a small bowl of very salty water

modeling clay

paper clips or coins

1. Mold the modeling clay into the shape of a small boat.

2. Put the boat in the bowl of fresh water.

3. Load the paper clips or coins in the boat one by one. Count how many it can hold before it sinks.

4. Now put the boat in the bowl of salty water.

5. Load the paper clips or coins in the boat one by one. How many can it hold before it sinks?

Floating liquids

Fresh water has a different density compared to that of salt water. In fact, all liquids have different densities.

How do you find out if a liquid is more or less dense than another liquid?

You will need:

a tall glass jar or bottle with a wide neck

a cup of water

a spoon

half a cup of syrup, such as corn syrup or maple syrup

half a cup of cooking oil

a metal coin

a toothpick

a piece of fruit

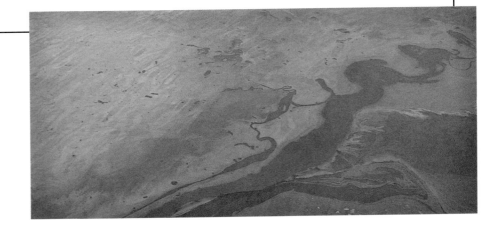

cooking oil

water

syrup

1. Pour the syrup carefully over the back of the spoon and into the glass jar. Then pour the water in the same way. Finally, add the oil. Which liquid is floating on top? Which is in the middle? Which is at the bottom? Can you describe how their densities differ?

2. Now, before you put the coin, toothpick, and piece of fruit in the jar, guess in which layer they will float.

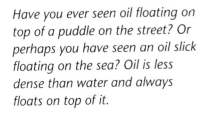

Have you ever seen oil floating on top of a puddle on the street? Or perhaps you have seen an oil slick floating on the sea? Oil is less dense than water and always floats on top of it.

Hard and soft water

Do you live in a place where the water is "hard"? It's easy to tell if you do. Hard water causes a chalky layer to build up inside a tea kettle in which water is frequently boiled. This chalky layer also builds up around the drain of a sink where water is often left standing. This layer is often called **scale**, **lime**, or **limescale**. Scientists call it **calcium carbonate**.

Water becomes hard when it soaks through soft rocks such as **chalk**, **limestone**, or **dolomite**. Chemicals from these rocks dissolve in the water. When the water is boiled, the dissolved substances change, leaving the solid calcium carbonate behind.

Limestone is a soft rock. A road has been tunneled through these limestone caves in the Pyrenees Mountains in France.

Scale and scum

In many ways, hard water is a nuisance. The minerals in hard water can build up in hot water tanks and pipes. In time, the tanks and pipes may become blocked. Also, when you wash in hard water, it is difficult to work the soap into a lather. Instead, the soap leaves an unpleasant layer of scum on the surface of the water.

For this reason, manufacturers add water-softening chemicals to laundry detergent. One of these chemicals is **sodium carbonate**, or **soda ash.** It removes the minerals that make the water hard and keep the detergent from cleaning properly.

Making hard water

Baking soda, or **sodium bicarbonate**, can make water hard. Here's how you can demonstrate the effect of hard water.

You will need:

two large bowls of water

baking soda

a spoon

soap

1. Dissolve several heaping spoonfuls of baking soda in one of the bowls of water.

2. Wash your hands with the soap in the bowl with the plain water. Can you work up a good lather? If you can, your water is not too hard.

3. Now wash your hands in the baking soda solution. Do you notice a difference? Why?

A car will rust if it is left out in all kinds of weather. Cars by the ocean are more likely to have rust damage. Do the experiment opposite to find out why.

The role of water in corrosion

What happens if you leave a shiny new iron nail out in the rain? In a day or two, reddish-brown spots will appear on it. The spots are called **rust.** In time, they will spread until they cover the whole nail. The nail has rusted.

What is rust?

When metals such as iron and steel are exposed to air and water vapor, the surface of the iron is changed into a chemical called **iron oxide.** Another name for iron oxide is rust. Rust does not stick closely to the iron and is not as strong as the iron. Air and water can work their way underneath rust and cause more rusting under the surface. It can gradually spread deeper into the metal.

Corrosion

When metals are affected by the action of chemicals, this is called **corrosion**. The rusting of nails and cars is corrosion. But not all corrosion is harmful. Moist air corrodes aluminum very quickly to make a chemical called **aluminum oxide**. Unlike rust, aluminum oxide clings close to the surface of the metal, and no air or water can work its way underneath. The layer of corrosion protects the metal.

Rusting

You can do some experiments to see what is needed to make rusting happen.

You will need:

four glass jars

water

cooking oil

salt

four iron nails

1. Put just enough water in one jar to cover the bottom. Put a nail in the water. The top should stick up above the surface.

2. Put a nail in the second jar with no water.

3. Ask an adult to help you boil some water to remove its air. Put enough of this water in the third jar to cover the nail completely—almost to the top of the jar. Pour a little oil on top to keep air out of the water.

4. Put just enough water in the fourth jar to cover the bottom. Before you put the nail in, stir plenty of salt into the water to make a strong salt solution.

What happens to the nails after a few days?

1. The nail will rust because there is air and water in the jar.

2. The nail will not rust very much because there is no water.

3. The nail will not rust very much even though it is in water, because the oil keeps out the air.

4. The nail will rust because there is water and air. The salt in the water speeds up the rusting, so the nail will rust more quickly.

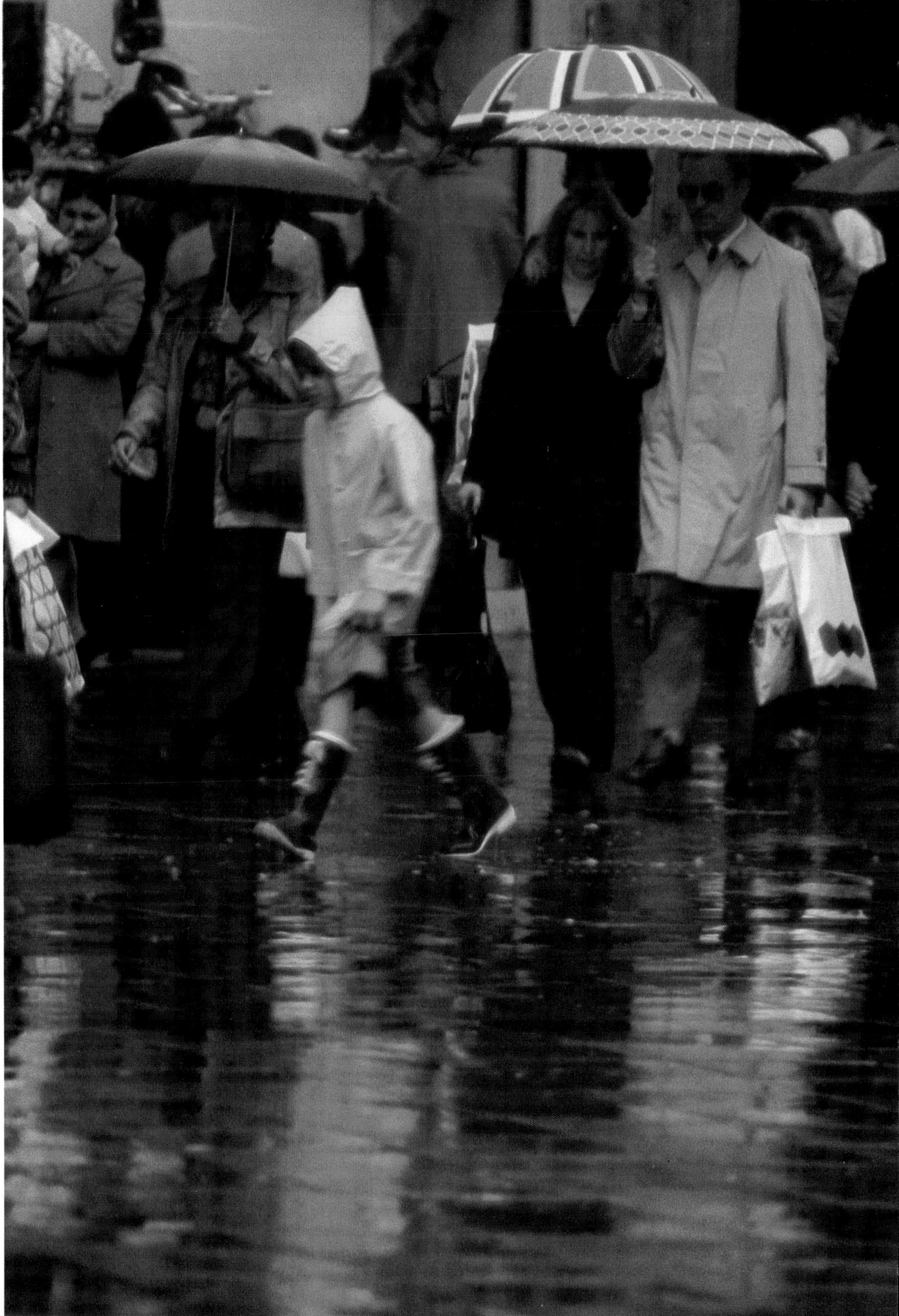

Keeping water out

We need water to live, but there are many places where we don't want it. One place where we don't want it is in our clothes. When we dress up to go out in wet weather, we wear clothes made of special materials that repel water. We say that these materials are **waterproof.** We also like to have leather shoes that are waterproof. Wood must be waterproofed when it is used for building houses or boats. These substances can be coated with rubber or oil, or any other waterproof substance. You can experiment yourself with waterproofing a substance.

Waterproofing

How can you stop an ordinary piece of cotton material from soaking up water?

You will need:

two small pieces of cotton material, about 2 inches × 2 inches (5 centimeters × 5 centimeters)

a piece of a candle

water

1. Set one piece of material aside. Take the other piece and carefully wipe the candle wax all over both sides. Make sure you don't miss any of it! This is easier if you use a colored candle.

2. Lay the two pieces next to each other on a table. Sprinkle them with drops of water.

The piece that you have not waxed will soak up the water. On the other piece, drops of water will stay on the surface and not soak in. Wax prevents water from soaking into the cotton.

Waterproof coats, boots, and umbrellas all help to keep us dry in the rain.

Squirt power

Firefighters are experienced at fighting big blazes. They are well trained and know how a fire will normally spread and how it can be brought under control. Most blazes are sprayed with powerful **jets** of water. It may take two firefighters to control each hose, as the water squeezes through the hose and bursts out of the nozzle at the end.

The hose is difficult to hold for two reasons. The force of the water as it pushes forward causes a strong backward force on the hose. The other reason is that when the water flows rapidly through a bend in the hose, it tries to straighten out the bend. This might cause the hose to jerk rapidly, making it difficult to keep a good grip. Firefighters have to grip hoses tightly in order to accurately direct the jet of water.

A firefighter sprays the blaze with strong jets of water. There is so much squirt power in the hose that the water can reach a fire as much as 100 feet (30 meters) away.

Newton and squirt power

Squirt power is an example of an important scientific law established over 300 years ago by the English scientist Isaac Newton. Newton found that when a force pushes in one direction, an equal force pushes back in the opposite direction. Newton called these two forces "action" and "reaction."

Fireboats

Have you ever seen a river fireboat? These boats patrol large rivers, ready to fight fires at warehouses, docks, and ships in port. They have powerful pumps that force river water through hoses, which they direct at the flames.

Fireboats sometimes take part in river carnivals. They make a fine display as they squirt water in all directions. At these times, they may use squirt power from the hoses to propel the boats through the water. The hoses are able to shoot water backward. This causes an equal force that pushes the boat forward.

A fireboat in New York squirts jets of water in a display of squirt power.

Gardeners' power

Gardeners often make use of squirt power to water their lawns. They use a rotating lawn sprinkler. When the water flows through the sprinkler, its forward force makes the rotating head move backward. This makes the sprinkler head turn, so that all the grass around the lawn sprinkler is watered.

Making water work

Have you ever seen a fast-flowing mountain stream? The water rushes along, sometimes carrying twigs and branches of trees with it. Sometimes, it is even strong enough to carry along rocks and boulders. Flowing water is a great source of energy. We can use water to make energy that will work for us.

Waterwheels

Thousands of years ago, people discovered how to make **waterwheels.** Some waterwheels had paddles around the rim, which turned the wheel as the water flowed into them. Others had buckets fixed to the rim. As each bucket filled with water, it became heavier and moved down. This pulled the wheel around.

Waterwheels were often connected to millstones to grind wheat or corn into flour. These machines were called **watermills.** Until about 200 years ago, watermills were used to drive machines in factories. After that, they were gradually replaced by engines powered by steam.

Energy from water

Today, the idea of the waterwheel is still used to provide energy. In **hydroelectric power stations**, water is used to drive a kind of modern waterwheel called a **water turbine.** The water comes from rivers and mountain streams. It is stored behind dams until it is fed through a pipe to the turbine. A dam with plenty of water behind it is an assurance that there is always a good supply of water to turn the turbine.

Water is stored behind the Kariba Dam in Zimbabwe. It flows out through the turbines, causing them to turn and generate electricity.

We also get energy from water in another way. **Geothermal power** is generated whenever water comes in contact with hot rocks below Earth's surface. The rocks give off heat that make the water hot enough to turn into steam. Power companies drill wells and pump the hot water or steam to the surface. The hot water or steam can then be used to generate energy.

Transport by water

For thousands of years, people have used water to transport goods. Boats and ships carry cargoes across the seas or along rivers. In some countries, logs can be moved from one place to another by floating them downriver.

This famous waterwheel at Hama, in Syria, has pumped water for irrigation for over 700 years.

Logs are floated downstream from the islands of Aland, in Finland.

Air pressure: Pressure caused by the weight of the air.

Ameba: One-celled organism.

Atmosphere: Air surrounding Earth.

Atom: Smallest part of a substance. An atom contains a mass of *protons* and *neutrons* in a center called a *nucleus* that is surrounded by electrons. Everything is made of atoms.

Catalyst: Substance that produces a chemical reaction in other substances without changing itself.

Climate: Pattern of weather over a period.

Condensation: Process by which a gas changes into a liquid.

Conduction: Flow of energy through a substance.

Continental drift: Slow movement of the continents.

Convection: Flow of energy from one place to another.

Convection current: Movement in the air that pushes water vapor from oceans and rivers into the air.

Core, inner: Earth's deepest and hottest layer.

Core, outer: Layer of Earth beneath the *mantle* and above the *inner core*.

Corrosion: Decay on metals caused by the action of chemicals.

Crust: Earth's hard, rocky covering. It consists mostly of two types of rock, granite and basalt.

Delta: Land area formed by clay and soil where a river meets the sea.

Density: The thickness or heaviness of a substance.

Desalination: Process of removing salt from seawater.

Dilute: To make weaker by adding water.

Erosion: Wearing away of rocks and soil by water, wind, and ice.

Evaporate: Process by which water turns into vapor.

Fault: Break in Earth's *crust*.

Fault-block mountain: Mountain formed when land is forced up through *faults* in Earth, creating a block-like shape along a fault.

Flash: When heated water turns quickly into steam.

Fold mountains: Mountains formed when plates in Earth's crust are pushed under one another, causing rocks to buckle up or fold.

Fossils: Imprints of remains of plants or animals, usually found in rocks.

Geothermal power: Power generated from hot water or steam that is created when water touches hot rocks below Earth's surface.

Geyser: Jet of boiling water and steam that bursts out of the ground.

Gravity: Force that pulls things toward Earth's surface.

Hydroelectricity: Energy created with water power.

Ice ages: Periods when ice covered large areas of North America and Northern Europe.

Iceberg: Huge chunk of ice floating in the sea.

Igneous rock: Rock formed when molten rock material cools and solidifies.

Ionosphere: A layer of Earth's atmosphere at the lower part of the thermosphere and the upper part of the mesosphere.

Irrigation: Bringing water to land that would otherwise be too dry for farming.

Limestone: Type of rock that is formed in layers over thousands of years.

Mantle: Layer of Earth beneath the crust and above the *outer core*.

Mesopause: The upper part of the *mesosphere*.

Mesosphere: The layer of Earth's atmosphere between the *stratosphere* and the *thermosphere*.

Metamorphic rock: Rock that has changed its appearance or its mineral composition due to intense underground heat and pressure.

Meteorologist: Scientist who studies the weather.

Molecule: Smallest unit remaining when a substance has been divided as much as possible without having undergone a chemical change.

Multistage flash distillation: A process of making fresh water by removing salt from seawater. Seawater is heated quickly in low-pressure chambers. The steam from the heated water is condensed into salt-free water.

Neutron: Tiny particle found in the nucleus of an atom. The number of neutrons found in an atom may vary.

Nucleus: Center of an atom. A nucleus is made of tiny particles called protons and neutrons.

Osmosis: Process whereby liquids move from one side of a skin, or membrane, to another. Liquids always travel from a weaker solution to a stronger one.

Ozone: Gas formed when ultraviolet rays from the sun change some of the oxygen in the *atmosphere.*

Porous: Having many small holes or pores that allow liquid to soak through.

Precipitation: Scientific word for rain, snow, hail, or sleet.

Reaction, chemical: Chemical action of two substances that results in the formation of additional substances.

Saturate: To soak a substance so thoroughly that it cannot hold any more of a solute.

Sediment: Small pieces of rock that are washed or blown away by water or wind.

Sedimentary rock: Rock formed when layers of older rocks, plants, or animals are pressed together over long periods.

Solar system: The sun and all the objects that travel around it.

Soluble: Dissolves in water.

Solution: Result of dissolving a substance, called a solute, in a liquid.

Stratopause: The upper part of the stratosphere.

Stratosphere: Part of the atmosphere where ozone is found.

Surface tension: Invisible "skin" on the surface of water made from water molecules clinging together.

Tectonic plates: Large sections of Earth that are part crust and part mantle.

Thermosphere: The layer of Earth's atmosphere that begins at the *mesopause.*

Tide: Changes in the level of water caused by the pull of *gravity* by the sun and moon.

Transpiration: Process whereby plants take in water from the ground and release it as moisture through their leaves.

Tropopause: Top part of the *troposphere.*

Troposphere: Part of the atmosphere nearest Earth's surface.

Volume: Amount of space taken up by a substance.

Page numbers in *italic* type are references to illustrations.

126 Acknowledgments

The publishers of **World Book's** *Young Scientist* acknowledge the following photographers, publishers, agencies, and corporations for photographs used in this volume.

Cover	© PhotoDisc, Inc.; © PhotoDisc, Inc.; © Douglas Faulkner, Photo Researchers
2/3	© PhotoDisc, Inc.
8/9	© ZEFA Picture Library
18/19	© Spectrum Colour Library
20/21	© Barr-Liaison from Frank Spooner Picture Library
22/23	© Pier Silvio Ongaro, Liaison Agency
30/31	© Timothy O'Keefe, Bruce Coleman Collection; © Dallas and John Heaton, Spectrum Colour Library
32/33	© Doug Allan, Science Photo Library
34/35	© Spectrum Colour Library
42/43	© J. H. C. Wilson, Robert Harding Picture Library
46/47	© ZEFA Picture Library
48/49	© Nicholas Devore III, Bruce Coleman Collection
50/51	© H. Bickel, ZEFA Picture Library
52/53	© Goebel, ZEFA Picture Library; © Jan Taylor, Bruce Coleman Collection; © Ian Murphy, Stone
54/55	© Ron Rieke, ZEFA Picture Library; © Ung Werbestudio from ZEFA Picture Library
56/57	© Black Star from ZEFA Picture Library
60/61	© Sarah Ermington, Hutchison Library; © R. Smith, ZEFA Picture Library
68/69	© Maroon, ZEFA Picture Library
74/75	© Artstreet
76/77	© Spectrum Colour Library
80/81	Buxton Mineral Water Company
84/85	© ZEFA Picture Library; © Carol Hughes, Bruce Coleman Collection
86/87	© Hutchison Library
90/91	© ZEFA Picture Library
92/93	© J. C. Allen, Frank Lane Picture Library
94/95	© Adam Hart-Davis, Science Photo Library; © A. J. Deane, Bruce Coleman Collection
96/97	© H. Eissenbeiss, Frank Lane Picture Library
98/99	© Stone
100/101	© F. Jack Jackson, Robert Harding Picture Library; © Spectrum Colour Library
102/103	© Spectrum Colour Library
104/105	© L. C. Marigo, Bruce Coleman Collection
106/107	© Spectrum Colour Library
108/109	© A. C. Waltham, Robert Harding Picture Library
110/111	© Mark N. Brultan, Bruce Coleman Collection
112/113	© ZEFA Picture Library
114/115	© Phil Hill, Robert Harding Picture Library
116/117	© Spectrum Colour Library; © ZEFA Picture Library

Illustrated by

Martin Aitchinson

Nigel Alexander

Hemesh Alles

Martyn Andrews

Sue Barclay

Richard Berridge

John Booth

Lou Bory

Maggie Brand

Stephen Brayfield

Bristol Illustrators

Colin Brown

Estelle Carol

David Cook

Marie DeJohn

Richard Deverell

Farley, White and Veal

Sheila Galbraith

Peter Geissler

Jeremy Gower

Kathie Kelleher

Stuart Lafford

John Lobban

Louise Martin

Annabel Milne

Yoshi Miyake

Donald Moss

Eileen Mueller Neill

Teresa O'Brien

Paul Perreault

Roberta Polfus

Jeremy Pyke

Trevor Ridley

Barry Rowe

Don Simpson

Gary Slater

Lawrie Taylor

Gwen Tourret

Pat Tourret

Peter Visscher

David Webb

Gerald Whitcomb

Matthew White

Lynne Willey